THE 100+ SERIES™

Reproducible Activit...

D1202739

Nonfiction
Reading Comprehension

Grades 5-6

by

Norm Sneller

Published by Instructional Fair
an imprint of
Frank Schaffer Publications®

Instructional Fair

Author: Norm Sneller
Editors: Jerry Aten, Sharon Thompson
Cover Artist: Jeff Van Kanegan
Interior Artist: Milton Hall

Frank Schaffer Publications®

Instructional Fair is an imprint of Frank Schaffer Publications.

Send all inquiries to:
Frank Schaffer Publications
3195 Wilson Drive NW
Grand Rapids, Michigan 49534

Nonfiction Reading Comprehension—grades 5–6

ISBN: 0-7424-0220-7

3 4 5 6 7 8 9 10 MAZ 12 11 10 09 08 07 06

Table of Contents

A Day in a Different World

Directions: Read the story and answer the questions which follow.

As in many places of the world, El Salvador, the small Central American nation bordering the Pacific Ocean, is home to both the wealthy and the very poor. The rich may live side by side with the impoverished who, if fortunate to find work, might serve as their gardeners and maids.

What is life like for a child from a poor home? Step into this setting.

A young boy might rise before sunrise to help light the wood stove in the corner of the family's one-room apartment in a dilapidated building called a *mesone*. He and his sister will be asked to carry the family's three-gallon plastic buckets to the neighborhood water station to fill them for the family's daily washing needs. When the children return home, they might breakfast on last night's corn bread or rice and a piece of fruit.

The mother of the family might wash their faces and straighten their hand-washed single set of school uniforms, which they wear daily to the local school. Perhaps the boy is fortunate, and his class has writing paper. Each student may have a half-sheet for working out math facts. Even though all students are required by law to attend school, many work to support their hungry families. In the boy's forty-student class of fifth- and sixth-year students, eleven children are unable to read or write.

At the noon break each child may eat what food he brought from home. The boy feels lucky if he has tortillas, rice, and beans. As a surprise, his mother might treat him with a rare piece of chicken or fish. Outside the school is a large dirt yard where children can play. Most boys, and some girls, too, play a pick-up game of *futbol* (what North Americans call *soccer*). Then it is back indoors for the children.

The boy learns many of his lessons by memory. The teacher states a fact, and students repeat the fact together. It is fun and rather common for the children and teacher to sing their lessons to one another.

After school, for the day ends at 2:30, the boy walks home. He has chores to do. Today he must join his father in cutting the grass outside the master's beautiful villa. He owns a machete with which he slices through the grass. His father is lucky. He is not only the groundskeeper and groom to the master's horses, but he also guards the master's property at night.

In the evening the boy will have fresh tortillas and beans, coffee, and on this day a warm bowl of vegetable and rice soup. By the end of this light supper, the only light in the home comes from the embers in the wood stove. The sun has set, and this home has no electricity.

The boy and his sister lay out their sleeping mats. They must get up at 5:30 tomorrow. Their mother lights a lamp. She embroiders a colorful design on the cotton cloth before her. She hopes to sell the cloth at the market so she can buy food and shoes for her family. Perhaps this weekend the boy will help her at the market. He might even earn money by carrying groceries for the rich. He goes to sleep.

1. What is *futbol*? _____

2. How does the family earn money? (name three ways)

   _____

   _____

   _____

3. How is this school different from yours? _____

   _____

4. What foods might the boy eat on this day? _____

   _____

   _____

5. Write a description of the boy's home, stating three facts. _____

   _____

   _____

6. If you could help the boy, what would you offer to assist him or his family?

   _____

   Why? _____

   _____

Home Sweet Home

Directions: Read the story and answer the questions which follow.

You were proud of that sand castle you made last summer at the beach. But perhaps you have noticed that we humans have much to learn from other creatures on this unique and awe-inspiring planet.

Take the termite. Human homeowners fear them. We call professional exterminators to rid our buildings of them. But they are great builders and planners. Each community builds a large home to last for as long as its colony exists. In a Nigerian termite community, each mound is built by one large—make that, very large—family of over a million members. The underground nests are topped by these mud mounds, which the working termites create using dirt and their own saliva. Mounds as high as twenty feet have been recorded. Inside the nests are fungus gardens, which must be kept at a temperature of 31 degrees Celsius. With no electric air-conditioning, these small creatures have designed their own air-flow system to keep their gardens safe and secure.

Wasps, unlike termites, must build new nests every year. Paper wasps chew wood with which they build "cells." As the number of cells increases (up to 15,000 in number), the wasps strengthen their building with woody struts. Inside the cells, eggs are laid, hatched into larvae, and grown into future generations of the family. The potter wasp, unlike her cousin, creates a mud "jar" nest for each of its eggs. To ensure an ample food supply, this mother stings caterpillars, paralyzing them. These living snacks are hauled into the jar nests, which are then sealed to protect the developing wasps.

Beavers prefer ponds as safe havens for their families. Ponds also serve as excellent roads by which to transport food into their homes. If no pond suits the adult beaver pair, they create one by constructing a dam. With ample water, beavers can create protected lodges of mud, sticks, and stones whose only entrances are submarine (below water surface). Each lodge, which may be two meters across, contains one living chamber. Supplies of food are kept in other "huts" or caches made of vegetation. Beaver, if undisturbed, may live in a lodge for many years.

Enjoy your sand castles but don't forget to marvel at the constructions of other creatures.

1. Behind each term below, mark T for termite, W for wasp, or B for beaver.

   a. mud _____
   b. sticks _____
   c. fungus _____
   d. saliva _____
   e. paper/wood _____
   f. underwater _____
   g. single entrance _____
   h. air conditioner _____

   i. 31 degrees C _____
   j. mound _____
   k. lodge _____
   l. caterpillar _____
   m. cell _____
   n. Nigeria _____
   o. sting _____
   p. yearly _____

2. Critical thinking: Why would a beaver pair wish to place their lodge entrance underwater?

   _____

   _____

3. Argue for or against: All termites should be exterminated from our human communities. _____

   _____

4. Find out: How long do you think a wasp lives? _____

5. Name one thing that you find impressive about each of the constructions of these creatures.

   termite _____

   wasp _____

   beaver _____

6. What is another amazing animal builder? _____ What do you appreciate about its constructions? _____

   _____

Name _____

My Little Runaway

Directions: Fill in the blanks with words from the bank to complete the sentences below.

What would you do to avoid becoming a meal for another animal? Perhaps you have not thought much about this. But many wild animals do!

1. In Central _____ one type of tree-hopper _____ itself to look like a green thorn.

2. The _____ tree-hopper of this species can fool its _____ by its brown, bark-like appearance.

3. The speedy antelope _____ high into the air as it _____ enemies.

4. This relative of the deer can *stot*, or leap, with all four _____ rising off the _____ at one time.

5. The king snake (red, black, yellow, black) looks so much like the greatly _____ poisonous coral snake (red, yellow, black, yellow) that preying birds stay _____ of it.

6. In a _____ manner, the sawfly, which in shape and color imitates the wasp, avoids attack, although it is a _____ insect.

7. But how _____ the five-lined skink? When in a _____ spot, its blue-colored tail can be broken off.

8. The tail twitches and _____, drawing the _____ of the predator until the lizard escapes.

9. The io moth confuses the enemy when it _____ its wings, _____ large, false eyespots.

10. Birds which instinctively _____ the eyes may take a _____ from the fur-like wing, but the wing-damaged moth may still escape.

Word Bank				
about	America	attack	attention	chunk
clear	disguises	earth	escapes	feared
feet	harmless	immature	leaps	predator
revealing	similar	spreads	tight	writhes

Name _____

Common Ground

Directions: Name the common issue of each word list.

Common Issue:

_____ 1. spade, rake, watering can, wheelbarrow

_____ 2. mutt, pooch, canine

_____ 3. Tokyo, Baghdad, Washington, D.C.

_____ 4. toe, sew, low, foe

_____ 5. soccer, football, lacrosse

_____ 6. moo, baa, neigh, chirp

_____ 7. solid, liquid, gas

_____ 8. Abby, Julie, Liz

_____ 9. meter stick, thermometer, graduated cylinder

_____ 10. red, blue, yellow

_____ 11. petunia, daisy, dahlia

_____ 12. frog, grasshopper, kangaroo

_____ 13. newt, frog, toad

_____ 14. Andes, Rockies, Alps

_____ 15. Monopoly, checkers, backgammon

_____ 16. mango, pineapple, banana

_____ 17. windy, cloudy, dry

_____ 18. harp, viola, guitar

_____ 19. Orinoco, Paraguay, Amazon

_____ 20. *si, da, ja*

hints: #3 not New York City; #4 not too; #5 not basketball; #8 not Ben; #10 not orange; #12 not mouse or snake; #13 not lizard; #15 not cards; #16 not strawberry; #18 not clarinet; #19 not Hudson; #20 not no.

Extra: Write your own list of words with a common ground. Test a friend to see if he or she can figure out your problem.

Name _____

Fascinating Facts

Directions: Underline the best word to complete each sentence below.

1. Try not to be too _____. The longest lightning bolt ever recorded was 32 kilometers long.
   happy   shocked   careful

2. Stalagmites are mineral _____ on cave floors. The tallest we know of, La Grande Stalagmite, is in France with a 29-meter height for now.
   wells   mines   deposits

3. How many earthquakes do we _____ per year? Try 500,000. Of these about one thousand are destructive.
   experience   create   chase

4. How fast can you travel? Because the earth spins entirely around every 23 hours, 56 minutes, and 4 seconds, a person standing on the _____ is speeding at 1,600 kmph.
   beach   equator   South Pole

5. Ever hear of Angel Falls? You can _____ this tall waterfall in Venezuela. It drops 878 meters (almost a kilometer).
   measure   show   observe

6. Is the earth a perfect _____? No. At the poles the earth is not as rounded as the rest of the planet.
   triangle   sphere   circle

7. There is an island in the Indian Ocean which has recorded the greatest one-day _____. La Reunion had 1.87 meters in 24 hours!
   waterfall   rainfall   nightfall

8. How _____ can it get? Travel to Algeria and find out. In 1973 land temperature there was raised to 59.4 degrees C.
   deep   cold   hot

9. How deep can we dig into the earth? So far, we humans have drilled down 9.58 kilometers. This hole is a _____ well in the state of Oklahoma.
   carbon dioxide   water   natural gas

10. You think the equator is a fast place? (See sentence #4.) Well, we all move faster than that at 107,200 kmph. You see, we zip around our star, _____.
the Sun   Alpha Centauri   Rigel

11. How high can you climb? If you are in great physical shape and have some free time, you might climb to 8,848 meters above sea _____. That's on Mount Everest.
coast   floor   level

12. How low can you go and remain above ground or water? At the edge of the Dead Sea in the _____ you will be 399 meters below sea level.
Atlantic Ocean   Middle East   Sahara Desert

13. The deepest part of the ocean lies in the Pacific Ocean. One spot has been _____ and is more than 11 km deep.
raised   measured   missed

14. What else is under the sea? Try volcanoes! Of 535 active volcanoes on the earth, _____ 80 are under water. Remember how the Hawaiian Islands were formed?
roughly   simply   mostly

15. It's cold outside! It was in Vostok, Antarctica, in 1983. There, the _____ dipped to -88.3 degrees C.
barometer   rain gauge   thermometer

16. Are you parched with thirst? You are not as thirsty as the Atacama Desert in Chile. In 1971 it received rain for the first time in 400 _____. Some regions in the Atacama missed that rain too!
years   days   months   centuries

Name _____

Shall We Dance?

Directions: Read the story and answer the questions which follow.

Let's travel. We are off to the farm belt in the great American Midwest. We will arrive on the fairgrounds of Cuming County, Nebraska.

It is summertime. People are showing off their wares, jams, jellies, baked goods, rides, and booths. Prize-winning cows, calves, boars, and sows are among the animals of all sizes and ages. But that is not what we have come to see. We are here for the exhibition dance.

This is a dance you probably will not see anywhere else. A few years ago, in 1997, some Nemaha, Iowa, residents sat down to discuss their town's one-hundredth anniversary celebration. Someone recalled a routine from the 1950s. Why not try it again? So they planned and practiced their fancy dance steps—without moving their feet. You see, they ride on eight vintage Farmall tractors painted a brilliant red. They promenade, mosey, swing, and thread their agricultural armor through complicated square-dance movements.

It was not easy from the start. The eight volunteer dance masters began with toy tractors on a kitchen table and soon realized that they would need assistance from a professional *choreographer*, a person who plans dance movements. A physical education teacher came to their rescue. Soon they were practicing difficult dance steps while walking through their formations, making tractor noises.

They have had their bumps and dings along the way. One broken hand and many bruises to both man and machine were part of the learning process. But now these eight, known as the Farmall Promenade, have requests to perform most every week. Not that they can always oblige. Many of the group are farmers, and it is difficult to get away from their farm chores.

With daring, colorful bravado, four men dress in bow ties and straw hats while the other four deck themselves in wigs, blouses, and gingham skirts.

Why are they willing to do this? Perhaps they like a good time. Perhaps it is their civic mindedness. Or, perhaps it is their need to smile. Farm prices are down. The weather has been hard on crops. The P.E. teacher-caller, Laurie Mason Schmidt, says, "We could stay home and whine. So it's a lifesaver to travel around and have fun together." And they certainly do!

May the fun continue!

1. Where does the story take place? _____

2. What is so unusual about this event? _____

3. If you were one of these dancers, what would you most fear? _____
   Why? _____
   _____

4. Why did the men first plan this activity? _____
   _____

5. Why do they continue to perform? _____

6. What is the "agricultural armor"? _____

7. Match these words and their meanings.
   _____ wares   a. cotton cloth
   _____ promenade   b. reckless bravery
   _____ bravado   c. goods
   _____ gingham   d. stroll

8. How else might people dance in a uniquely new manner? _____
   _____
   _____

Name _____

Birds of a Feather

Directions: Use the clues and scrambled letters to find the names of the following birds. Use reference materials if you need help.

Clues	Scrambled Letters
1. nests on chimney tops, returns to same place every year **name** _____	OKTRS
2. attracts female bird with its nest, nest begins as looped grass which is woven and knotted to tree branches **name** _____	DAIRVWRBEE
3. attracts female mate with "treasures" with which it lines its stick home. If attracted to a male, the female will make a cup-shaped nest nearby. **name** _____	DIROWREBB
4. makes nest on the ground; nest is made of mud, bits of vegetation and hair, lined with grass. nest is dome-shaped, entrance on side. **name** _____	NEBVDORI
5. nest is covered with lichens, is two inches in diameter, and held together with spider silk **name** _____	UYBR-DARTTOEH DGIMHUBIRMN
6. lines its nest with pebbles and shell pieces; nest is only a scrape in beach sand **name** _____	GIIPPN EVOLRP
7. nests on cliffs; very little lining in nest. sometimes uses abandoned eagle's nest. **name** _____	REPGEIERN CLAFNO
8. nest hangs from tip of tree branch; a woven bag of bark, plant fibers, and string **name** _____	HERONNTR ILOORE

Name _____

Thirst Quenchers

Directions: Use the pictures below to name twelve thirst-quenching liquids.

1. _____   [map] - M + L + [spider] - P

2. _____   [lemon] + ADE

3. _____   H + [pan] - P + [tube] + O + [plate] - P

4. _____   [ice] + [water spray]

5. _____   [lock] - K + [bear] + E + J + [triceratops] - M

6. _____   [mouse/rat] - M + [mouth] - TH

7. _____   4 - F + [ruler] + J + CHEWS - CH

8. _____   [golf putt] - T + [ruler] - IN

9. _____   GR + [gorilla] + S + [frog] - T + A

10. _____   [bacon/meat] + [fly] + R

11. _____   [sneezing man] + [feet/socks] - T

Name _____

Earth Shakers

Directions: Fill in the blanks below with words from the word bank to complete the article.

On the earth certain areas of the crust are relatively thin or even broken. Here the hot rock within the earth may 1. _____ its way out.

When this happens, we have a volcano.

The hot 2. _____ within the earth is called *magma* when it has become so hot that it liquifies. If this 3. _____ hot rock escapes through cracks in the crust and rises above ground, we call the liquid *lava*.

Volcanoes act in 4. _____ ways. Some volcanoes pace themselves slowly, visible first as smoke rising from the earth.

But sometimes volcanoes may present themselves violently and 5. _____ through the earth's crust with showers of rocks, 6._____, and toxic gases.

Some volcanoes arise out of the sea. In such cases, steam and smoke may 7. _____ from the ocean surface. Lava, boiling from the undersea crust, 8. _____ and illuminates the water with an eerie 9. _____.

Long ago a volcanic 10. _____ destroyed the city of Pompeii in today's Italy. It moved so rapidly that people and animals were 11. _____ and covered with the liquid rock which then cooled, enclosing them in its rock-hard coffin.

In the middle of the past century, a Mexican volcano was born. It grew 12. _____. On its second day, it rose to 13. _____ times a man's height. After seven days it was 150 meters high. The volcano grew and grew. In one year it had buried a 14. _____ town whose church tower was the 15. _____ survivor. The former village and the volcano are named Paricutín.

Word Bank

ascend	ash	captured	different
eruption	explode	five	flowing
force	glows	light	nearby
rapidly	rock	sole	

Name _____

Geography Gems

Directions: Match the terms from the word bank with their meanings. Use a dictionary if you need help. Draw a picture to illustrate each term.

Word Bank				
bay	island	isthmus	plateau	peninsula
lake	escarpment	tributary	plain	

1. a large area of flat or gently rolling land

term: _____

2. a steep cliff about 100 stories high

term: _____

3. water surrounded by land

term: _____

4. land surrounded by water

term: _____

5. a large, mostly flat area that rises above the surrounding land

term: _____

6. a stream or river which flows into a larger river

term: _____

7. land with water on three sides

term: _____

8. a part of a sea or lake that extends inland

term: _____

9. a narrow strip of land that connects two larger land masses

term: _____

Directions: Match the terms from the word bank with their meanings. Use a dictionary if you need help. Draw a picture to illustrate each term.

Word Bank				
strait	pass	mouth	fauna	flora
canyon	mountain	cataract	delta	

1. a large waterfall; a strong rush of water	2. a gap between mountains	3. a triangular-shaped plain at the mouth of a river
term: _____	term: _____	term: _____
4. a narrow stretch of water that connects two larger water masses	5. the animals of a region	6. the plants of a region
term: _____	term: _____	term: _____
7. an area that rises steeply at least 2,000 feet above surrounding land	8. the point where a river enters a lake or sea	9. a deep, narrow valley with steep sides
term: _____	term: _____	term: _____

Name _____

Starting with D

Directions: Read each definition below and write the word, starting with D, that fits with each definition. Find and circle the 21 words in the word search puzzle below. Use a dictionary if you need help.

1. a maiden _____

2. to drench with water _____

3. to move rhythmically _____

4. a precious stone _____

5. to stain _____

6. to put on _____

7. a male duck _____

8. loose earth _____

9. canine _____

10. moist _____

11. an oblong, sweet, fleshy fruit _____

12. a one-humped camel _____

13. mournful _____

14. a common American wildflower _____

15. a risk _____

16. two-fold _____

17. a fine, woven table linen _____

18. uncertain _____

19. a short race _____

20. a lack of rain _____

21. twelve of a kind _____

```
L U F T B U O D O D
E C N A D D A I S Y
S D R O M E D A R Y
M D N A E D E M D L
A A L U F E L O D A
D S E T A D D N O U
D R K U N Y D U D D
D A O S T E O N S R
H T N U A G Z E E A
S D R G G M S Z D K
A Y U I E H A O D E
D A M P D R T D C D
```

Name _____

Victorious

Directions: Read the time line to complete the story web below.

1940—Wilma Rudolph is born in Clarksville, Tennessee. She weighs four pounds. She has nineteen older brothers and sisters.

1945—At the age of five, Wilma contracts scarlet fever and polio. This leaves her with a left leg that is twisted inward. News spreads that she will never walk again.

Childhood: Although unable to walk, Wilma exercises. The nearest hospital willing to treat black people is 50 miles away. The local school will not accept her because of her disability.

Childhood: She is able to obtain a steel leg brace from the hospital. She can now go to school. Still she is unable to play with others. She exercises on her own.

Childhood: One Sunday as Wilma and her family come to church, Wilma removes her leg brace and walks without help.

1952—Wilma is able to take off her brace for the last time. Wilma and her mother mail the brace back to the hospital.

Teens: Wilma begins to play basketball. She had studied and memorized the moves of this game while watching classmates earlier.

Teens: In high school Wilma leads her team to the state championships. They lose in the finals. A college coach scouts the state final, and Wilma is given an athletic scholarship to attend the university and participate in track and field.

1960—Wilma represents the United States in the Olympic Games. She wins the gold medal in both the 100-meter and 200-meter events, despite a twisted ankle. Her 400-meter relay team also wins a gold medal.

1962—Wilma Rudolph becomes a second-grade teacher and a high school coach.

1994—Wilma Rudolph dies.

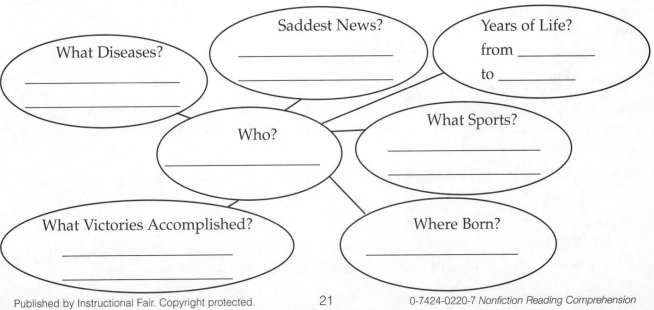

Scribbling Master

Directions: Read the story. Then answer the questions on the next page.

Theodore Geisel was born in Springfield, Massachusetts, on March 2, 1904.

His father was a beer maker until the United States passed a law in 1920 making all production of alcohol illegal. His father then worked part-time in zoos and parks. Theodore often visited him and sketched what he saw.

Geisel went to college and he graduated in 1925. He then traveled to Oxford, England, to study.

In 1927 he married Helen Palmer. They toured Europe together and then returned to the United States. He worked in advertising for fifteen years.

Geisel wrote his first book for children, an alphabet book, which no one would publish. However, in 1937 a friend published his book *And to Think That I Saw It on Mulberry Street*. Geisel gave his name as Dr. Seuss. Seuss was his mother's maiden name.

During World War II he wrote scripts for war documentaries and drew cartoons. He held the army rank of captain.

In 1948 Geisel and his wife, Helen, moved into their new home in California. An old watchtower on his property became his studio and office.

In the 1950s Geisel was challenged to write a book for children using no more than 250 words. In 1957 he published *The Cat in the Hat,* using only 220 words.

Next, a friend bet him fifty dollars that he could not write a publishable book using a mere 50 words. In 1960 *Green Eggs and Ham* was published. He never accepted the money from the bet.

After Seuss traveled to Hiroshima, Japan, and witnessed the horrors of nuclear weapons, he wrote *Horton Hears a Who.*

The book which took Dr. Seuss the least time to write was *The Lorax.* He wrote it on a laundry list in forty-five minutes. This was the only book of his which some people tried to ban. The logging industry feared that Seuss would hurt its trade.

During his lifetime Dr. Seuss received a Pulitzer citation, an Emmy award, and an honorary doctorate degree. On his birthday he sometimes received as many as 20,000 birthday cards from his fans.

He died on September 24, 1991.

1. Name three of the books written by Dr. Seuss.

   _____

   _____

   _____

2. What structure became his studio? _____

   _____

   _____

3. Name something which influenced his writing. _____

4. During World War II, what did Geisel do? _____

   _____

5. What do you like best about his work? _____
   Why? _____

   _____

6. How do these terms fit with his life?

   220 words _____

   Hiroshima _____

   "Seuss" _____

   logging_____

Name _____

My Children Are Hungry

Directions: Read the events from the life of Sitting Bull. Then determine whether each of the statements at the bottom is true or false.

This great Native American was born in March 1831 in what is presently the state of South Dakota. He was born to the Western Sioux tribe.

When he was young, this man was called Slow by his people. He never seemed to be in a hurry. However, at the age of 14 his father renamed him *Tatanka Iyotake*, or Sitting Bull, when he showed outstanding bravery in a battle with the Crow people.

As a young man, Sitting Bull was considered a prophet. He foretold many events which would come to his people. It was during this time in the mid-1800s that white people came across the plains in large numbers, heading for the fertile lands of the far west. They killed many buffalo, sometimes for food and sometimes for sport. The loss of buffalo was hard on Sitting Bull's people, who depended on buffalo for their lifestyle.

The United States signed a peace treaty in 1868 with the Sioux nation. Sitting Bull refused to sign it or to live on the reservation assigned to his people. He did not believe that the government in Washington, D.C., would abide by the treaty. Two years later the United States did break the treaty, and war broke out between Native Americans and U.S. soldiers. Sitting Bull and his people fled to Canada.

However, complaining that his people were hungry, Sitting Bull and the Sioux threatened to return to their homeland, and they did. On June 25, 1876, a battle ensued between the Sioux, including Sitting Bull, and General George Custer's army. This was the last major victory of the Sioux people.

Sitting Bull died at Wounded Knee, South Dakota, on December 29, 1890.

Write T for true and F for false.

_____ 1. Tatanka Iyotake means "buffalo skin."

_____ 2. Sitting Bull was born in the present state of Oregon.

_____ 3. Sitting Bull refused to sign the peace treaty in 1868.

_____ 4. He was present at a battle against General Custer's army in 1874.

_____ 5. Sitting Bull was a member of the Chippewa tribe.

_____ 6. The Native Americans became upset when whites killed their dogs and cats.

_____ 7. Sitting Bull died at the age of 59.

_____ 8. He never left the state of South Dakota.

_____ 9. He fought the Crow people at age 14.

_____ 10. The Sioux considered Sitting Bull to be a prophet.

The Inca

Directions: Read the article and answer the questions that follow.

The Inca were an Indian people of South America who, at one time, ruled one of the largest and richest empires in the Americas. The Inca began as a tribe or group of tribes in the area of Cusco. Not much is known of the Inca until after 1200 when they began to expand their rule over neighboring peoples. The Inca empire began around 1438, when Pachacuti, the ninth Inca ruler, quelled an invasion by their neighbors, the Chanca. Pachacuti was both an able administrator and a skilled military leader. He conquered many regions and rebuilt the city of Cusco, in southern Peru, as the center of his empire. The empire eventually extended over 2,500 miles (4,020 kilometers) along the western coast of South America. It included parts of what are now Argentina, Bolivia, Chile, Colombia, Equador, and Peru. The empire ended in 1532 when the Inca were conquered by the Spanish.

The Inca were skilled in many areas, especially in engineering and handiwork. They built a vast network of roads that linked distant provinces and constructed suspension bridges that spanned rivers and canyons. Their buildings were of skilled construction and great size. The Inca designed fine articles from gold and silver, made beautiful pottery painted with geometric designs, and wove fine cloth. They often used these fine cotton and woolen fabrics, made from llamas and alpacas, as a medium of exchange.

Even though many of the Inca were fine craftsmen, the majority were farmers. Despite the fact that they did not use wheels or plows pulled by animals, their system of farming was advanced. In the desert, they built an irrigation network. In the hills, they cut terraces that reduced erosion and aided in irrigation. The main crops of the Inca included corn, cotton, potatoes, a grain called *quinoa*, and an edible root known as *oca*. All family members worked together in the fields and at other tasks.

The people lived in extended family groups that included more than one generation. Most lived in small, thatched-roof houses made of adobe or stone set in mud. In contrast, nobles lived in large, richly decorated stone palaces.

The major means of travel was by foot. People and llamas carried anything that needed transporting. Nobles rode in litters, a framework fitted with couches, that were carried on men's shoulders. The people used boats and rafts on major rivers.

The Inca spoke a language called *Quechua*. They had no written language. Messages were passed by messengers stationed along roadways and by fire and smoke signals. Since the common people did not attend schools, children learned by watching and imitating their parents as they worked. Children also learned by listening to the stories told by their elders. Noblemen's sons went to school in Cusco for four years. They studied the Inca language and religion. They learned history by listening to the poems and legends recited from memory by their teachers called *amautas*. The boys also learned how to fight and to keep records on the *quipu*, a cord with knotted strings of various colors and lengths.

The Incas predicted the seasons of the year by studying the stars and planets. They also performed mathematical calculations in order to design buildings, roads, and terraced fields. Inca musicians played drums and woodwind instruments, including flutes, panpipes (an instrument made of a series of pipes or reeds of graduated length bound together), and trumpets made of ceramics and shells. Inca priests played a major role in the Inca community. They were responsible for religious ceremonies as well as for treating the sick.

Information about the Inca has been gathered from well-preserved archaeological remains. These tell us much about the life and history of the Inca. We can also learn about the Inca from the written records of the Spanish during and after their conquest of the Inca. Though the Spaniards tried to put an end to their customs, the Inca heritage still can be seen today in the language, medicinal practices, clothing, and farming methods of the Indians in the highlands of Peru and other countries where the Inca once reigned.

1. Who were the the Inca? _____

_____

_____

2. What present-day countries were once part of the Inca empire?

_____

_____

3. List three main crops of the Inca.

_____

4. Write two or three sentences about the family life of the common people.

_____

_____

_____

5. Name two areas in which the Inca were skilled.

_____

6. Match the words with their definitions.

oca	a teacher
Quechua	an edible root
amauta	the spoken language of the Inca
quipu	a musical instrument
panpipe	a cord used to keep records

Name _____

A Young Maiden

Directions: Read the selection and answer the questions which follow.

Joan was a farmer's daughter in France. While still quite young, she said she heard voices from heaven. Throughout her teenage years, the voices spoke to her often. She was convinced that God wanted her to force the English out of her country. Here is a time line of events.

1412   Joan of Arc is born.

1413   The English defeat the French at Agincourt.

1424   Joan reports speaking to the archangel Michael for the first time.

1428   The French king is under English attack in the city of Orleans.
Joan goes to Vancouleurs, where she begs for soldiers so she may save the French king.
Joan cuts her hair short, an unheard-of thing for a woman of this time to do.

1429   Joan meets the French king. Joan's army defeats the English at Orleans.
Here the English commander, William Glasdale, drowns in the river.
The English believe Joan to be a witch.
The French king is crowned. Joan's family is raised to the rank of nobility.

1430   Joan's army rushes to save Compiègne. Her French allies abandon her.
Joan is captured and brought to the city of Rouen.

1431   Joan is put on trial at Rouen and charged with heresy.
She is burned at the stake.

1920   Joan of Arc is canonized.

1. What was Joan's age (estimate) when
    a. the French king was crowned?   _____
    b. the English defeated the French at Agincourt?   _____
    c. Joan's army saved Orleans?   _____
    d. the angel voices first spoke to Joan?   _____
    e. Joan was burned at the stake as a heretic? _____

2. The Burgundians, a French people, assisted Joan's enemies. What nation was Joan's enemy? _____

3. What happened at Rouen? _____

4. Who is Michael? _____

5. In what town did Joan cut her hair? _____

6. Why might the English have believed that Joan was a witch? _____

_____

Name _____

The Shona

Directions: Read the story and match each term on the following page with its correct description.

Long ago, there was an important culture in the region between the Zambezi and Limpopo Rivers. These were the *Shona*. This group came into the region of southern Africa before the year A.D. 1000. The Shona spoke a common *Bantu* language and all were herdsmen and farmers of the land, but their customs and religious beliefs varied. By the 1300s they had expanded their political organizations from villages or clans into empires. These new countries frequently clashed with one another over trade with the Arab and Portuguese merchants. Articles of trade of the Shona region included gold and ivory.

Mapungubwe, an ancient city by the Limpopo River, was a center for Bantu traders and craftspeople more than one thousand years ago. Because it was built over a plateau surrounded by cliffs of sandstone, Mapungubwe could be reached only by climbing a rope. Historians believe that a millennium ago, its inhabitants brought up 2,000 tons of soil so that the settlers could farm outside the city on the plateau. The people of Mapungubwe crafted pottery and gold artifacts. They traded with the distant lands of India and China. So, why haven't we heard of this city? During the restrictive years of *apartheid*, the South African government wanted the world to believe that white colonists were the first humans in the region. For 70 years, the government hid the truth. But black Africans had settled the country many centuries earlier.

The present-day country of Zimbabwe receives its name from a Bantu word, *zimbabwe*, which means "stone building." The Great Zimbabwe is one of many stone-walled fortresses built on the Zimbabwean plateau. Researchers believe that the Shona people built this large stone structure over a course of 400 years. More than 18,000 people might have lived in the Great Zimbabwe. Their lives centered on cattle raising, agricultural products, and gold trade. But sometime around 1450–1480, the once-powerful city-state was emptied. Perhaps some day we will learn why.

Another ancient stone city has only recently been discovered. Thulamela, in South Africa's Kruger National Park, was uncovered about ten years ago. The Shona people built it 800 years ago. It was still active when the Plymouth Colony in America held its first Thanksgiving feast. The people of Thulamela were miners, makers of steel tools, and traders. Today, the site is open to the public.

Match the words to their definitions. Then fill i

_____ 1. Bantu

_____ 2. Great Zimbabwe

_____ 3. Kruger

_____ 4. Mapungubwe

_____ 5. millennium

_____ 6. plateau

_____ 7. seventy years

_____ 8. Shona

_____ 9. Thulamela

_____ 10. trade

_____ 11. two thousand tons

_____ 12. vacated

_____ 13. Zambezi

_____ 14. zimbabwe

a. a r

b. a r

c. st

d. a

e. a

f. 1

g.

h. how long a sect

i. only reached by rope

j. home to 18,000 people

k. emptied, disappeared

l. the language of the Shona

m. exchange of goods between people

n. how much soil was lifted up cliff side

terminology

Directions: Circl
correspond to
single word

1. W

Name five accomplishments of the Shona people.

1. _____

2. _____

3. _____

4. _____

5. _____

Look Closely

...e the correct choice for each question below. Rearrange the letters which ...he correct answers to fill in the blank at the bottom of the page with a

...ich of these must a plant have to live?
   sand—F   pebble—A   sunlight—V   river—H

2. Which direction do all rivers flow?
   north—C   south—T   downstream—S   downwind—J

3. Which one is a star?
   Bantu—W   Alpha Centauri—B   Tibet—A   Bali—X

4. Which animal is a marsupial?
   squid—A   squirrel—W   kangaroo—O   rabbit—S

5. Which of these is not a force?
   structure—I   gravity—V   magnetism—C   centrifugal—E

6. Which of these does not name a musical instrument?
   cymbal—O   powder horn—N   ukulele—M   piano—U

7. Which of these inventions influenced the industrial revolution most?
   barbed wire—C   laser—K   steam engine—T   radio—O

8. Which of these colors is not composite?
   red—E   orange—M   green—R   violet—A

9. Which of these is not a mammal?
   whale—U   giraffe—G   dog—D   snake—O

10. Which of these was not a scientist?
    Laura Ingalls Wilder—R   Jacques Cousteau—H   Marie Curie—E

11. Which of these is a muscle?
    nose—E   heart—A   hair—R   teeth—F

We gain much of our scientific knowledge through careful _____.

Name _____

Pick Three

Directions: Circle the three words that share a common idea. Then write a phrase to explain what they share with each other.

1. longitude   equator   latitude   orbit
   Commonality: _____

2. sleet   wind   rain   hail
   Commonality: _____

3. South America   Asia   South Africa   Europe
   Commonality: _____

4. Spain   Oahu   Sri Lanka   Sicily
   Commonality: _____

5. Sudan   Tanzania   Pakistan   Angola
   Commonality: _____

6. Bangkok   Danube   Orinoco   Euphrates
   Commonality: _____

7. Atlas   Shield   Ural   Sierra Madre
   Commonality: _____

8. tree   iron   river   army
   Commonality: _____

Name _____

Which "-ist" Is It?

Directions: Circle the term which corresponds with each definition. Each term will be used one time only.

1. one who studies bacteria
   cyclist   bacteriologist   optometrist   soloist

2. one who studies forces in the universe
   dentist   flutist   physicist   meteorologist

3. one who studies the development of the human race
   optimist   chemist   arborist   anthropologist

4. one who studies living things
   medalist   geologist   biologist   pianist

5. one who studies the composition of all matter
   chemist   florist   botanist   linguist

6. one who specializes in the science of matter and energy
   specialist   physicist   colonist   medalist

7. one who studies human behavior
   bacteriologist   purist   cellist   psychologist

8. one who specializes in the care of trees
   rigorist   arborist   biologist   optimist

9. one who expects a favorable outcome
   optimist   linguist   optometrist   dentist

10. one who is trained to offer eye care
    anthropologist   optometrist   geologist   florist

11. one who studies the earth's structure
    psychiatrist   geologist   physicist   chemist

12. one who plays a large four-stringed instrument
    sociologist   purist   medalist   cellist

Name _____

A Blast from the Past

Directions: Read the following story and place the events on the next page in order.

Imagine that you are out in a wilderness. It is a quiet summer morning. The early morning sky is clear. Suddenly you hear a deafening roar and the earth shakes beneath you. You are bounced up into the air, and when you return to earth, you are knocked unconscious by the powerful blast. Some time later you awaken. What you see is the evergreen forest burning. Many scattered fires smoke and crackle around you. What happened?

An event like this actually occurred in Russian Siberia at the turn of the century. A tremendous explosion was heard and felt at 7:17 a.m. on June 30, 1908. From data collected by Russian scientists and from eyewitnesses, we are able to piece together the story with some certainty.

What was it? A stone meteorite, probably 50 to 60 meters in diameter, that exploded into millions of dust particles, small stones, and rock fragments as it smashed into Earth's atmosphere at a speed somewhere between 12 and 20 kilometers per second. The meteorite broke apart roughly 6 kilometers above Earth. Eyewitnesses saw "a ball of fire" or "a flying star with a fiery tail," "a pillar of fire," "a cloud of ash on the horizon." Its vibrations were recorded by sensitive instruments 1000 kilometers away. At 500 kilometers' distance, observers heard "deafening bangs" and saw a fiery cloud. Nearer still, witnesses described a sunlike fireball. At 60 kilometers, windows broke, jars fell from shelves, and people were tossed to the ground.

What damage resulted from the blast? Unlike the opening of this piece, the explosion occurred over an uninhabited wilderness area. The nearest humans to the blast were reindeer herdsmen who, at 30 kilometers from the landing, felt the impact. One herder was thrown about 40 feet through the air and struck a tree. His is the only recorded human death from the blast. Certainly many woodland animals were killed. But the wilderness forest was blasted. After the blast, there was silence. Directly below the blast, bare tree trunks whose branches were stripped away stood as mute reminders of the damage. But even trees at a distance of roughly 5 to 15 kilometers were blown over. Blasts of heat which rushed from the meteorite were so hot that they set small fires in many parts of the wilderness.

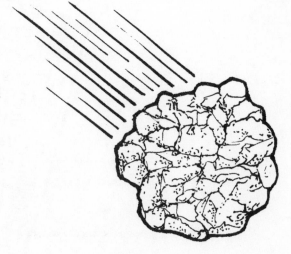

Put these events in the order in which they occurred. Start with 1 for the first event.

_____ a silence follows

_____ herdsmen are knocked unconscious

_____ trees are tossed to the ground

_____ the meteorite smashes into the atmosphere

_____ an explosion of light fills the area

_____ the vibrations and light can be seen 500 kilometers away

_____ with a roar the meteorite bursts apart

Directions: Write T for true and F for false. Change false statements to make them true.

_____ 1. A comet caused this blast.

_____ 2. We know of only one human death resulting from this event.

_____ 3. The damage was caused when the space object hit the earth.

_____ 4. The blast was heard early in the afternoon.

_____ 5. Tree trunks were left standing beneath the blast.

Name _____

Canada

Directions: Number each section of events in chronological order.

Canada has a long and interesting history. Here are some events and milestones that are important to the development of this North American country.

Northwest Territories

_____ In 1789 Alexander Mackenzie traveled down a huge river which now bears his name.

_____ Then around A.D. 1000, it is possible that Norse adventurers bumped ashore.

_____ In 1999, the Northwest Territory became two territories—Nunavit and Denedeh. The former is a self-governing Inuit community.

_____ It was first settled more than 12,000 years ago by ancestors of the Dene Nation.

_____ One hundred and twenty years ago, Great Britain gave up the islands of the Arctic to Canada.

_____ On his mission to find a route to China, Martin Frobisher landed here in 1576.

Yukon

_____ In 1825, Great Britain and Russia signed a treaty. Great Britain obtained the Yukon while Russia received Alaska.

_____ Work began on the Alaska Highway in 1942, and Whitehorse became the new capital city of the Yukon Territory.

_____ In 1896, the Royal Canadian Mounted Police arrived with twenty-two men to keep order as the gold rush began.

_____ Whaling in the Beaufort Sea finally ended in 1914 when whale oil was no longer needed.

_____ In the mid-nineteenth century, fur traders and missionaries arrived.

_____ Even before the Europeans came, Native Americans became infected with their diseases through trade goods.

_____ Within three years of the gold rush, Yukon became a federal territory.

Newfoundland and Labrador

_____ France, Portugal, and Spain all fished at the Grand Banks in the late fifteenth century.

_____ For thousands of years, Inuit people hunted here.

_____ In 1867 Newfoundland decided not to join the new country of Canada. It was an independent country for many years.

_____ England claimed St. John's Isle in 1497.

_____ The colony was ruled by fishing admirals from 1634–1832.

_____ Bjarni Herjolfsson was blown off course and landed here more than 1,000 years ago.

_____ In the mid-twentieth century, Newfoundland joined Canada as its tenth province.

Name _____

Cruising Along

Directions: Fill in the blanks with words from the word bank. Each word should be used one time.

1. The first engine-powered road vehicles were _____-driven, but the internal combustion engine was much more practical. Between 1900 and 1910, hand-built cars could only be afforded by the _____.

2. With the mass production lines of Henry Ford in Detroit, Michigan, cars were brought down a line to the _____, each responsible for _____ simple task. Production-line cars could be built quickly, which made them much more affordable for ordinary people.

3. In Germany, a _____ car called the _____ was built. Its name means "people's car."

4. The combustion temperature inside an engine's cylinders can reach 3000 degrees Fahrenheit. To keep the engine _____, most cars use a water-cooling system.

5. Air-filled_____ gave cars a more comfortable ride than the early, solid _____ tires. The first electric _____ for cars arrived in 1905 to _____ gas lanterns.

Word Bank

cool	headlights	one
popular	replace	rubber
steam	tires	Volkswagen
wealthy	workers	

Name _____

In an Orderly Fashion

Directions: Below are four topics. Match each sentence with the appropriate topic by writing the code letter in the correct blanks.

Topics: A   The Shakers: a religious group that once flourished in America
          B   Carpetbaggers: white Republicans who traveled South after the Civil War
          C   Harry Houdini: a famous American magician
          D   Mount Rushmore: a monument in South Dakota

_____ 1. This was built to a scale as if the men were 465 feet tall.

_____ 2. He became a trapeze artist at the age of 8 years.

_____ 3. He even starred in silent movies.

_____ 4. This work of art was begun in 1927 by Gutzon Borglum.

_____ 5. Some taught and worked with post-war freed slaves.

_____ 6. He was extremely strong and agile.

_____ 7. Many carried their possessions in old pieces of carpet.

_____ 8. They were very popular before the Civil War.

_____ 9. It was carved on granite cliffs.

_____ 10. He was born in Budapest, Hungary.

_____ 11. It was finished by the creator's son in 1941.

_____ 12. Mother Ann became a leader in this movement.

_____ 13. Many were prosperous businessmen.

_____ 14. The group was begun by two ex-Quakers.

_____ 15. Some bought up abandoned plantations.

_____ 16. It is the tallest statue in the world.

Name _____

How Revolutionary!

Directions: Read each revolutionary article. The four statements which follow are not all true. If false, write F. If true, write T. Place an asterisk in the blank by the true statement which states the main idea.

1. To pay off its national debts, the British government increased the taxes paid on its products by its colonies. The American people who were subjects of Great Britain at this time wanted nothing to do with this taxation. They considered it very unfair. So, during the night of December 16, 1773, a rowdy band of Bostonians acted up. Dressing as Mohawk Indians, they climbed aboard three merchant ships in the Boston Harbor. They hoisted 342 chests of tea and merchandise into the harbor.

   _____ Bostonians Dress as Native Americans

   _____ Great Britain Taxes Colonies Fairly

   _____ Tea Is Dumped into Harbor

   _____ Native Americans Angered by Treatment

2. The setting is Paris in the summer of 1789. Citizens were fed up with paying high taxes to King Louis XVI. While nobles and church leaders got richer and richer and paid no taxes, commoners worked from dawn to dusk for meager wages. French citizens gathered into a riotous mass. Some of the men broke into the royal armory and took muskets. Then the angry group gathered outside the Bastille, the king's fortress prison. The group attacked the Bastille, took all of the gunpowder stored there, and freed the prisoners. Louis XVI, who had ignored the demands of the working class, may well have wished he had listened more closely to their demands.

   _____ Louis XVI Listens Well

   _____ The French People Revolt

   _____ The Bastille Is a Fortress Prison

   _____ Nobles Pay High Taxes

3. World War I was hard on the Russian soldiers. The winter snows had closed many of the rail services. The people of St. Petersburg were running low on flour and coal. They had little to eat and could not heat their houses. On February 23, International Women's Day, a large crowd of women gathered to protest these harsh living conditions. More and more women came, leaving their factory jobs to show their support of protesters. More than 100,000 women marched. When the Russian soldiers were ordered to turn them aside, they refused. Later that week, the marchers protested again, this time with men joining the women. Army officers and the police were ready. As the rioters advanced, shots were fired and civilians fell. But people kept marching forward. Suddenly, the soldiers, ignoring their orders once again, joined the protesters. They destroyed the police stations and defied Tsar Nicholas II and his government.

_____ Soldiers Join the People

_____ Women Meet on International Women's Day

_____ The Police Defeat the Women of Moscow

_____ Women Work in Factories

4. In 1934, in the heavily populated country of China, an event took place that is called the March to Freedom. The various regions of China fought one another for control of the land. The Communist Red Army, 100,000 strong, was nearly surrounded by its heavily armed adversaries, the *Guomindang*. The Red Army escaped in one long, fast-moving line, but during its long flight, the army was under constant attack. In less than three months, its number had dwindled to 40,000 soldiers. It took a year for the army to flee to the northwest province of Shaanxi. In the end, only 8,000 reached safety. Then a new war started between the attacking Japanese and the Guomindang, forcing the Guomindang back to the eastern provinces. The Red Army took this time to reorganize and build up its ranks.

_____ Japan Attacks China

_____ China Defeats Shaanxi

_____ The Red Army Barely Survives March

_____ The Guomindang Lose 960,000 Soldiers

Name _____

Women Rule!

Directions: Here are five women who have made a difference in the world. After reading each article, label it with the correct vocation title: doctor, painter, pioneer, poet, or ruler.

Laura Ingalls Wilder, 1867–1957, is well known for her "Little House" series of nine children's books. Laura Ingalls was born in Pepin, Wisconsin. She and her family moved from place to place and lived a rugged pioneer existence. Her first book, *Little House on the Big Woods*, is based on her childhood experiences. In 1885, Laura married Almanzo Wilder. *Farmer Boy* tells about his childhood. Laura's books follow her life from childhood to marriage. These books have been applauded for the picture they present of the American frontier.

_____

James Barry, 1795–1865, was really Miranda. In the nineteenth century, women were not permitted to become doctors, so Miranda Stuart disguised herself as a man and changed her name in order to take classes in medicine. While we know little of her background, we do know that she graduated as a doctor when she was 17. She served as an army hospital assistant and eventually became inspector general. That is the highest rank doctors could achieve. For fifty years she kept her secret. She served in Europe, the Americas, and Asia. Only after her death was her secret discovered.

_____

Salote Mafile'o Pilolevu, 1900–1965, was born on the island of Tonga in the southwest Pacific. She went to New Zealand for her education, returned to Tonga where she married at the age of 17, and ascended the throne one year later. During her long reign, Salote worked hard for the people of her land. Education, health, living conditions, and Tongan culture were all special concerns to this monarch. She wished especially to improve the welfare of her nation's women. This remarkable queen, generous to her people, is a model for us all.

_____

Wang Yani, 1975– , was born in a small town in southern China. Her father, an art teacher, recognized her interest, potential, and talent very early in her life. Her first art exhibition was held in Shanghai when Yani was only four years old. Yani paints using traditional Chinese materials, but her style of broad brush strokes, says her critics, is refreshingly unique. She enjoys listening to music while she works.

_____

This young African girl was taken from the Fula people in western Africa and was shipped to Boston in 1761. This kidnapped child was given the name Phillis Wheatley by her new owner, Susannah. Unlike many slaves of the time, Phillis was taught to read and write. She began her studies of Latin when she was 12. Because of her obvious display of intellect and poise, Phillis was encouraged to speak in the homes of Boston's educated leaders. Her poetry especially interested her hosts. Phillis became a world-recognized writer at the age of 17. She was the first African-American author to have a book of poetry published. She met General George Washington in 1774. At the death of her mistress' husband, John Wheatley, in 1778, Phillis became a free woman.

_____

Directions: Match these terms with the correct woman.
Women: Miranda   Phillis   Salote   Laura   Yani

1. slave _____

2. China _____

3. author _____

4. culture _____

5. army _____

6. Pepin _____

7. Tonga _____

8. disguise _____

9. American frontier _____

10. George _____

11. women's rights _____

12. Boston _____

13. brush strokes _____

14. children's books _____

Name _____

Do You Believe?

Directions: Read the following paragraphs and answer the questions that follow.

In sixteenth-century England, people believed that if you saw your double in a mirror, you might die. This presence, known as a *fetch,* may have been so named because it had come to fetch you to another life beyond death. People who claimed to see a fetch said it stood behind you, was only visible in a mirror, and did not appear to be breathing. Interestingly, many people who claimed to see fetches were those who were or had recently been ill, and had been weakened by fighting off disease.

1. What did the English call a person's double? _____

2. How did people claim to see this presence? _____

_____

John Rudell, a British clergyman, wrote about an incident in his journal in 1665. A young boy had to cross a meadow each day to go to school. Every day, he said he was met by a pale ghost who did not walk upon the earth but floated above it. When the boy described the ghostly female, his father claimed she must be a family friend who had died three years earlier. Rudell, to whom the father told this tale, asked to go with the father and the son the following day. Rudell wrote that the three met the ghost and asked her why she had come. She whispered that a sickness would destroy England within a year. She disappeared and was never seen again. In the following twelve months, the great plague of London struck; over 70,000 people died.

3. Who was John Rudell? _____

4. Who saw the ghost first? _____

5. What did she warn? _____

_____

It was World War II. Sergeant Alex B. Griffith, an infantry sergeant, was leading his patrol along a French country road. All was peaceful; no danger was expected. A figure appeared in the road ahead, silently motioning Griffith to halt his column. Strangely, no other soldier saw this figure—a double of Griffith himself. Shaken and baffled by his hallucination, Sgt. Griffith halted his men. An army vehicle drove past his resting men, and shortly afterward the sound of machine gun fire rang out. The truck driver had been killed. Griffith believes that he was warned by this mysterious visitor. In 1964, Alex Griffith and his family took a hike through the woods when suddenly, from around a bend in their path, the 1944 Sergeant Griffith double appeared, waving and wordlessly motioning Alex to stop. Again, no one else saw the apparition. Griffith commanded his family to turn around and go back. Within seconds, a good-sized tree crashed down across the trail. Had the family gone on, they would have been crushed.

6. What did the ghost look like? _____

7. How did the warning figure seem to save Griffith?

   1944 _____

   1964 _____

8. What does the word *column* mean here? Circle the correct answer.

   a weapon   a news article   a tall pillar   a line of soldiers

Name _____

Fact or Fiction

Directions: Use words from the word bank to fill in the blanks in the article below.

According to stories of the ancient past, the Yeti is a creature which 1. _____ in the Himalayan countries of 2. _____ and Tibet.

Yet many people in 3. _____ times have wondered if such a creature 4. _____ exist. When an English expert 5. _____ workers to capture unusual creatures in the Himalayan mountains in 1832, they 6. _____ to his 7. _____ with frightening stories of an encounter with a creature much like the 8. _____ beast.

9. _____ prints found in the snows of the land were 10. _____ and large, but they could have been made by bears or even people. Yet some of these 11. _____ were very large—some nearly 24 inches long and six inches 12. _____.

Perhaps the strangest 13. _____ comes from a Captain d'Auvergne who, when injured 14. _____ alone in the mountains, claims to have been 15. _____ by a 16. _____ -foot-17. _____ beast which carried him to its shelter, 18. _____ him, brought him back to 19. _____, and let 20. _____ go. What would this creature have been?

Some Yeti findings are 21. _____ false—rocks which looked human-like, bears mistaken for the 22. _____ beast, captured Yeti-skin souvenirs later determined to be of a rare 23. _____.

But is it possible that Yeti 24. _____? The 25. _____ has yet to be found to make a solid case.

Word Bank				
account	antelope	camp	certainly	exists
fed	Foot	furred	health	him
hired	lives	might	modern	mythological
Nepal	nine	prints	proof	rescued
returned	tall	unusual	while	wide

Name _____

Space Missiles

Directions: Read the following and answer the questions which follow.

Read these notes about three types of space rocks.

Comets
- Ancient people believed that they foretold terrible events.
- We know of hundreds of comets.
- A comet has an icy core and is covered with black dust.
- Comets look like large, dirty snowballs.
- Sunlight causes the gas cloud *coma* to glow.
- The coma's gases are always directly away from the Sun.
- Comets are usually a few miles wide.
- Most comets travel in elliptical oval orbits around the Sun.
- We see bright comets only once or twice every hundred years.

Meteoroids
- They can be seen every day.
- Millions of them exist.
- Although they are sometimes called shooting stars, they are really bits of rock or metal and are smaller than comets.
- When they enter Earth's atmosphere, they glow brightly and are called meteors.
- The glow results from friction with Earth's atmosphere.
- Meteors come much closer to Earth than comets.
- Very bright meteors are called *fireballs*.
- A meteor shower happens when Earth passes through an old comet orbit.
- A meteorite is a meteoroid that lands on Earth's surface.

Asteroids
- These are the largest of the space rocks.
- Many are found in a space belt between the orbits of Mars and Jupiter
- We know of about 3,000 asteroids.
- Some are a few miles across; one is much larger . . . 600 miles in diameter!
- If an asteroid hits Earth, a huge crater may be formed.
- Perhaps the extinction of dinosaurs resulted from such an impact.

1. Place the space rocks in order by size, smallest to largest. _____
   _____

2. Place them in order by numbers known, smallest to largest. _____
   _____

3. What superstition centered upon the sighting of comets? _____

4. What causes the brightness of these rocks? a. _____

   b. _____

5. What is a fireball? _____

6. Distinguish these terms:

   meteoroid _____

   meteor _____

   meteorite _____

Name _____

The Adventurers

Directions: Read the story and answer the questions which follow.

In his book *Over the Top of the World*, Will Steger relates the travels of his research party across the Arctic Ocean from Siberia to Canada in 1994. With a team of six people and thirty-three dogs, Steger set out by dogsled to complete this daring mission. Along the way, the party would exchange dogsleds for canoesleds because of the breaking ice packs.

Why did the team choose to go on this adventure? We may assume that these six individuals were voyagers who were thrilled by challenges. The difficulty of such a crossing was enough reason for them. But they also opened up educational links with classrooms around the world on the Internet. With computer and satellite technology, they could send news about their discoveries, their position, and their story on every day of this four-month journey. A third goal of Steger's team was to investigate the advance of air- and water-borne pollution to the Arctic northland.

The human team members were a multinational force. The original six included a Russian physicist, an American teacher-dogsledder, a Japanese journalist, a British explorer-musher, a Danish army officer, and Steger, the American coordinator-adventurer. The team was transported to their Siberian drop site by helicopter. Already in the first days of the mission in mid-March, one team member, after nearly freezing to death following a rescue of his dog team in the broken Arctic ice, had to quit the mission and return home. A replacement joined the five remaining teammates for the final three-week leg of the Arctic crossing.

With the departure of one human and his eleven dogs, the travelers divided the remaining twenty-two sled dogs into three groups of seven or eight. The dogs pulled their 800-pound loads using a tandem hitch. This hitch style pairs up dogs along one main pull line. The largest and strongest dogs are placed nearest the sled. They are known as *wheel dogs*. The one or two dogs at the front of each tandem line are specially trained and are very intelligent. They are the *lead dogs*. All remaining dogs of the team paired along the tandem length are called *team dogs*. Every dog had gone through much training. They were chosen to participate in this adventure both because they loved to pull loads and because they have proven their physical ability. Each dog was given a daily ration of a specialty food. Each two-pound block of packed nutrition contained 6,000 calories.

What were some of the major problems along the way? Certainly the cold was a constant threat. Wind chills can drop the cold factor to negative 80 or 90 degrees Fahrenheit. Any skin exposed to the cold air could end up frostbitten. The team, who researched this planned mission well, was surprised by the snowfall they witnessed. Such heavy snow was unexpected and slowed them down. Because the journey was over frozen water, the travelers were in constant fear of cracking ice and of becoming separated from one another. However, with their excellent technological equipment, the team never needed to worry about becoming lost. They could call for help if the need arose. Like their dependable dog mates, the humans were required to eat well to remain strong and healthy and were ordered to consume 5,000 calories apiece each day. Remember how the team had to travel over ice? Sometimes while they struggled to move across the perilous icy sheets for miles in one direction, the ice platform flowed in the opposite direction! This held them back and sometimes discouraged them. The sledders had to go over or around the many large ridges of ice blocking their way. They sometimes trudged miles out of their way when breaks appeared in the ice.

With three weeks remaining, the human team was met by its last supply plane. This rendezvous called for the departure of their twenty-two sled dogs and the arrival of three canoes and the party's newest teammate. With no dogs to help, the human pairs had to at times pull the 500-pound loads across the ice. At other times, they boarded their canoes to cross chilly stretches of water. They worked from 9 a.m. until 9 p.m., breaking for ten minutes every hour and resting from 2 o'clock to 4 o'clock. Day in, day out, they inched forward to their final resting point—land. Finally, on July 3, their journey, which had started on March 9, came to a close.

1. What happened and how did it happen? _____

   _____

2. Who participated? _____

   _____

3. Where did the story take place? _____

4. When did this journey happen? _____

5. Why did the team undergo this mission? _____

   _____

6. Use a dictionary or thesaurus to give definition to these words:

   tandem _____

   rendezvous _____

7. In 10–20 words, answer this question: Would you be interested in an
   adventure like this? Why or why not?_____

   _____

   _____

Name _____

More Adventures

Directions: Below are three problems. All of them relate to the story of Will Steger's Arctic adventure on pages 46–47. Choose one problem. Respond to it in the space provided.

1. Imagine: One team member left when he saw that the mission was so dangerous. Mr. Steger did not criticize him for leaving. Why might this be?

2. Argue for or against this statement: The training of dogs for dogsled adventures is cruel and unnecessary in today's world environment.

3. List: If you were a reporter sent to interview the team members of the Arctic adventure after their trip, what questions would you ask? Create a list of six to eight questions.

_____
_____
_____
_____
_____
_____
_____
_____
_____
_____
_____
_____
_____
_____
_____
_____
_____
_____
_____

Name _____

Adventure Matchup

Directions: Place a letter in each blank provided to match the two parts of each sentence below. All of the sentences relate to the story of the Arctic adventure on pages 46–47.

_____ 1. Because they had layers of fur . . .

_____ 2. To eliminate extra weight from their loads . . .

_____ 3. With Will's Global Positioning System computer . . .

_____ 4. The team collected snow samples for scientists . . .

_____ 5. Early one morning the team awoke hearing a grinding, thundering roar . . .

_____ 6. Because the ozone layer has almost vanished in the Arctic . . .

_____ 7. The food was placed inside waterproof duffel bags . . .

_____ 8. When one traveler fell into the deep waters of the ocean . . .

_____ 9. With winds so strong . . .

_____ 10. Because the loaded dog sleds were very heavy . . .

_____ 11. When one dog was frightened badly . . .

_____ 12. To keep the computer (named Charlie) from freezing . . .

a. he was completely coated with ice.

b. team members covered their faces entirely with sunscreen.

c. so it wouldn't become soggy even if tipped into the ocean water.

d. the team of huskies were insulated against the arctic cold.

e. to discern amounts of air-borne pollutants.

f. the team could see how far it traveled each day.

g. as a 20-foot-high wall of ice came rushing toward camp.

h. he was permitted to sleep in the tent of his master one night.

i. one could get frostbite on the face even when sweating from exertion.

j. Julie heated a hot-water bottle and slipped it inside its bag.

k. the team cut towels in half and removed the handles of their toothbrushes.

l. the teams could travel only slowly at first.

Name _____

From the Animals

Directions: Use the chart to answer the riddles on the following page.

Origin	Old Name/ Characteristics	New Name/ Characteristics	Additional Information
Asia	Wolf hunted in packs; competed with humans for food	Dog was trained for guarding, hunting, and herding	still gathers into packs when circumstances allow
Africa	Wild Cat 4,500 years ago was captured when its ability to hunt rats in Egyptian granaries was discovered	Domestic Cat has been trained to fish and hunt; can survive well on its own	A trait it continues to possess is its love of solitary hunting.
India/ China	Red Jungle Fowl was first domesticated 4000 years ago; normally lays 30 eggs a year	Chicken through breeding techniques and special foods can produce up to 300 eggs per year	Even after millenniums of life with us, this animal has a pecking order as it determines its position in the flock.
Ukraine	Przewalski's Horse probably captured about 5,500 years ago	Horse has gone through many changes because of breeding practices	first domesticated as a beast of burden
Middle East	Wild Bezoar Goat along with sheep was one of the first domesticated animals perhaps 10,000 years ago	Goat still milked like cows in some countries	also raised for meat and hides
Forest	Wild Boar could live on almost anything edible; 12 young to a litter	Pig now weighs twice as much as its ancestor; 20 young per litter	easy to raise; good source of meat
Eastern Hemisphere	Auroch lived in herds; domesticated some time later than sheep and goats	Cow still today it fights within herd for dominance	raised for meat, skin, horn, milk, and fat
Himalayas	Yak could live in high, cold regions with thin air	Yak a sturdy pack animal	raised for its meat milk, hide (for tents), wool

1. My ancestors come from the Middle East. What am I? _____

2. Imagine, 300 per year. What am I? _____

3. My hide is so thick one could make a tent from it. What am I? _____

4. I eat almost anything. What am I? _____

5. We were trained to fish and hunt. What am I? _____

6. My species still tends to gather into packs. What am I? _____

7. Like my ancestors, I use the pecking order. What am I? _____

8. We are solitary hunters. What am I? _____

9. I come from the Russian Ukraine. What am I? _____

10. The auroch is my ancestor. What am I? _____

Name _____

Say What?

Directions: Fill in each of the blanks with the letter that identifies the correct choice of word.

Creatures of the animal world are able to communicate with one another in many ways.

1. The firefly, a night-flying beetle, _____ to its own species by _____ of a flashing light . . . in code!
        a. territories   b. means   c. tail   d. signals

2. Octopuses are known to change color to _____ their peculiar moods. The color _____ denotes fear.
        a. hear   b. female   c. express   d. white

3. Certain honeybees talk to one another in _____. A figure-eight movement _____ that the food source is more than 80 meters distant.
        a. dance   b. more   c. distinctive   d. shows

4. Scientists have _____ six specific facial expressions in wolves, _____ expressions of friendliness and playfulness.
        a. means   b. including   c. dance   d. identified

5. A cat swishes its _____ before it attacks its _____.
        a. prey   b. attract   c. white   d. tail

6. When a _____ moth is ready to mate, it will release a tiny amount of perfume. Even a few _____ of this scent will tell a male moth where to reach his love.
        a. molecules   b. heard   c. mark   d. female

7. Whales, who communicate by singing, may be _____ a distance of up to 1200 km away! The songs, which may last a half _____, are sung only by unmated males.
        a. hour   b. vegetarian   c. heard   d. prey

8. The male lemur will _____ a malodorous fragrance from a special gland in his arm to his tail. This he waves in the _____ of a rival in a showdown.
        a. rub   b. including   c. express   d. face

9. Members of the dog family _____ their _____ with small doses of urine.
        a. territories   b. mark   c. signal   d. molecules

10. Elephants, who talk to each other through bark, roar, and rumble, can _____ each other as _____ away as 8 km.
         a. face   b. shows   c. hear   d. far

Name _____

It's Yukigassen Time!

Directions: Read the following and answer the questions which follow.

In April 2001 the Finnish sponsored the International Snow Battle Contest. To get more details you may wish to contact the Kemijärvi Tourist Office. But here's some of the scoop on this multinational event.

Team: The team includes one captain and nine registered players. There are seven active players and two substitutes on a team. The captain may join his/her team as a player. In the beginning there must be seven players on the field, at least three of whom must be women. Seventy-two teams are accepted to participate in the Snow Battle Contest.

Duration: The standard time of one period is three minutes. Three periods make up one game. The first team to win two periods wins the entire game.

Costumes and Flag: The team must wear similar costumes (not white). The team flag must be made of cloth. Its height is 50 centimeters and its length 1 meter. The flagpole length must be 1.5 meters.

Equipment: Helmets with head and face protection are required. They are handed out by the organizing agency. No spiked shoes are permitted.

Rules:
- When a player is hit by a snowball, he or she must leave the competition field.
- A team may win a period if
  a. the winner snatches the enemy's flag, or
  b. the winner has a larger number of living fighters at the end of a period.
- Nobody may protest against the decisions of the referees.
- Each team makes its own snowballs.

Prizes: The winning teams receive prizes, along with winners in the following categories: best team flag, best costume, best fair-play team, best cheering team.

1. How can a team win this game?
   a. _____ .   b. _____

2. How long might a game take? _____
   How short might a game be? _____

3. Name three friends you would want on your team. Describe what characteristics would make them valuable to your team.

   _____   _____
   _____   _____
   _____   _____

4. How can you tell that this snow fight competition is light-hearted and friendly?
   _____

5. Design a flag for your team on the back of this page.

Name _____

Spring to Life!

Directions: Match these terms with their descriptions. Use resources such as the encyclopedia if you need help.

Ancient people thought much of the season of springtime. To them the renewal of the earth made the difference between life and death.

1. _____ vernal   a. king of the underworld

2. _____ equinox   b. goddess of spring

3. _____ Eostre   c. he was held captive every winter by evil spirits

4. _____ Demeter   d. season of spring

5. _____ Hades   e. goddess of earth and agriculture

6. _____ oak trees   f. sacred objects of the Druids

7. _____ Celtic sun god   g. equal day and night

Read this synopsis of the following Greek spring myth:

Long ago, the wise and bountiful goddess Demeter lived with her lovely daughter Persephone. Where they dwelled the world was at peace. The earth produced plenty, and mortals had no want for food. Children were born and raised. Men and women thanked the gods.

But the powerful Hades saw the beautiful Persephone. He wished to make her his wife. Knowing that Demeter would never allow the departure of her daughter, Hades kidnapped the young maiden and fled with her to his underground home.

In her sadness Demeter ignored her work. The trees, the crops, the bushes and grasses—indeed, all plants of the earth—perished. Mortals cried out in grief and in fear, asking the gods for aid.

Hearing the pleas of these men and women, Zeus demanded a compromise. Persephone would return to her mother's side every spring. There she would remain for six months. The earth would renew itself. But for the other six months, she must return to her husband Hades. This is the reason we have the seasons.

True or False:

_____ 8. Demeter died each year.

_____ 9. Zeus cared for mortal men and women.

_____ 10. Plants died each year.

_____ 11. Hades married Demeter.

12. According to this story, why do we have six months of plant growth?

_____

Name _____

We Are Their World

Directions: Unscramble the letters to identify these terms below.

We have many tiny beings living on and around us. Some are very helpful. Others can make us ill.

1. an individual living thing

   ASMIGONR

   _____

2. a group of living things living closely together

   YNOOLC

   _____

3. special proteins made by the immune system to kill germs

   ABDEINITSO

   _____

4. any organism that cannot be seen with the naked eye

   ECIBRMO

   _____

5. microorganisms that cause diseases

   EOAHGSPTN

   _____

6. a mixture of bacteria and saliva that forms on teeth

   EQLPUA

   _____

7. an organism that lives off another without benefitting its host

   SIAETARP

   _____

8. although it includes all microorganisms, we usually label disease-causing bacteria and viruses by this name

   RMEGS

   _____

9. the place or environment in which a plant or animal normally lives

   BATTAIH

   _____

10. a tiny creature living off dead human skin; one of the most numerous animals in the world

    DSTUTIME

    _____

11. a one-celled animal in the protozoa family

    AABEMO

    _____

12. poisonous substances produced by plants, animals, or microbes

    NIXOST

    _____

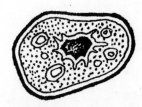

Name _____

Measure for Measure

Directions: Unscramble the words in the sentences below to read about measurements past and present.

1. bushel A four equals pecks

   _____

2. pace a have and two Walk steps you

   _____

3. is A measure the fingers across palm hand of your four

   _____

4. holds bits memory byte of eight A

   _____

5. is 45 English ell long The inches

   _____

6. meters comprised An are square hundred is one of

   _____

7. fingertip the cubit is to distance from A elbow

   _____

8. is it the orbit the earth the A year Sun to takes time

   _____

9. became one's of one The width thumb inch

   _____

10. width A digit one's finger is of the

    _____

11. paces a was Roman mile thousand A

    _____

12. equals A league miles three

    _____

13. water liter one of weighs A kilogram

    _____

14. approximately year six is light miles A trillion

    _____

Name _____

True Stories from the Sea

Directions: Here are six short descriptions of animals from under the ocean. Can you match each with a title that fits its description?

Titles: What Big Eyes You Have!   Breathe Deeply
          Keep Out of the Light   Dill Pickle
          The Cadillac of Fish

The anglerfish lures its prey with a part of its fin which serves as its fishing pole. This fin, located between the eyes of the anglerfish, emits a small light which glows from the very tip. When a curious shrimp checks out this light, he is promptly devoured.

_____

Few large sharks are found in deep sea water, but that is where the megamouth shark resides. It swims with its mouth wide open, feeding upon the tiny plankton which migrate through its territory. This huge fish is as long as a large automobile. Discovered in 1976, the megamouth's scientific name is translated as "giant yawner of the open sea."

_____

The kraken is a giant squid. While no healthy kraken has ever been seen or photographed, scientists believe it may grow to 57 feet in length. Squid have ten long tentacles covered with toothed suckers. These help the creature hold its prey. The kraken also possesses a hard, sharp beak for crushing its victims. This keen-sighted creature has the largest eyes of all earth's animals . . . almost 18 inches in diameter! _____

The deep sea cucumber is not a plant! It's an animal. This creature, which can live 30,000 feet below the ocean surface, is about the size of a pickle. And it reminds some people of a bumpy-backed piglet. It gets its food by sucking or chewing mud from the ocean floor.

_____

The elephant seal can hold its breath for a long time. With its huge lungs and specialized circulatory system, this mammal can remain underwater for one hour at a time. Typically it may spend 20 hours each day below the surface of the water. It dives deep to eat squid. Possibly it spends much of its time in the depths to avoid its rival, the great white shark.

_____

deciphering

Name ______________________

Northern Language

Directions: The Vikings used runic symbols in their writing. Try this playful activity to determine the English names for objects the Viking people knew. Be patient—not all words are spelled as we would spell them today. Use the key below for help.

1. ____________________ means of travel ᛒᚬᛏ
2. ____________________ everyday tool ᚴᚾᛁᚠ
3. ____________________ food source ᚴᚬᚢ
4. ____________________ settled island ᛁᛋᛚᛅᚾ
5. ____________________ ornamental fastener ᛒᚱᚬᚬᛏᛋᚼ
6. ____________________ demanded of enemies ᚴᚬᛁᚾ
7. ____________________ what France gave them ᚾᚬᚱᛘᛅᚾᛏᛁ
8. ____________________ means of travel ᛋᚴᛁ
9. ____________________ Viking heaven ᚠᛅᛚᚼᛅᛚᛚᛅ
10. ____________________ food source ᚠᛁᛋᚼ
11. ____________________ Viking letters ᚱᚢᚾᛋ
12. ____________________ popular red-bearded god ᚦᚬᚱ
13. ____________________ home-building material ᛏᚢᚱᚠ
14. ____________________ bread grain ᛒᛅᚱᛚᛁ

Now try writing your name in runic letters.

ᚠ	ᚢ	ᚦ	ᚬ	ᚱ
f	u	th	o	r
ᚴ	ᚼ	ᚾ	ᛁ	ᛅ
k	h	n	i	a
ᛋ	ᛏ	ᛒ	ᛘ	ᛚ
s	t	b	m	l

Name _____

The Explorers

Directions: Read the story and answer the questions which follow.

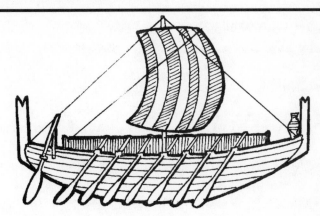

The Phoenicians were excellent sailors and explorers. They lived in the land of present-day Lebanon. As they developed and promoted a system of sea trade across the Mediterranean region, they also set up many colonies along the Mediterranean coast. One very famous colony, Carthage, became the main base for trade, exploration, and colonization.

A Carthaginian admiral of the fifth century B.C. named Hanno led an important voyage along the western coast of Africa. Before his expedition, people of the Mediterranean knew nothing of this part of the world. Loading the ships of his flotilla with food supplies, trade goods, and hopeful colonists, Hanno set sail and passed the Straits of Gibraltar.

Six Phoenician colonies were established along the coast of present-day Morocco. Journals were kept describing the people, the land, and the animals discovered. Hanno wrote of dense tropical forests, erupting volcanoes, enormous blazing lights (probably grass fires on the plains), and hairy savages (likely baboons or chimpanzees).

Hanno, the early explorer, advanced mankind's knowledge of the earth.

1. Draw a line between these terms and their descriptions.

   a. journals   land of ancient Phoenicia
   b. Carthage   where six colonies were established
   c. Lebanon   admiral
   d. Hanno   famous colony
   e. baboons   written records
   f. Morocco   hairy savages

2. At what skill were Phoenicians very good? _____

   _____

3. Where does Hanno's journey lead him? _____

   _____

Name _____

Turn the Radio On

Directions: Read over the notes below and place them in chronological order.

Guglielmo Marconi made a big contribution to modern life.
Here are notes about his life, placed in chronological order.

• Guglielmo Marconi was born in 1874.

• He received private education until he entered the Livorno Technical Institute.

• Heinrich Hertz discovered and created radio waves in 1888.

• Marconi read an article written in 1894 that proposed that radio waves could replace the telegraph for sending messages.

• Marconi practiced with radio waves and could send and receive signals two miles.

• He took out a patent on his invention in 1896.

• The British navy began to use Marconi's instruments on some of its ships.

• Marconi sent a message 31 miles across the English Channel in 1899.

• In late 1901, the inventor transmitted a radio message across the Atlantic Ocean.

• In 1909, he was awarded the Nobel Prize in physics for his discoveries.

• Guglielmo Marconi died in 1937.

1. Number these pieces of information in order:

    _____ private education   _____ British navy   _____ read article   _____ born

    _____ Atlantic Ocean   _____ two miles

2. Number these pieces of information in order.

    _____ patent   _____ Nobel   _____ died   _____ Livorno

    _____ Heinrich   _____ English Channel

3. Write one sentence which captures the essence of this inventor's achievement.

    _____

Name _____

Fantastic Fungi

Directions: Circle the correct letter in each if-then statement below. Then fill in the blanks to the puzzle which follows. You may need other resources to help you.

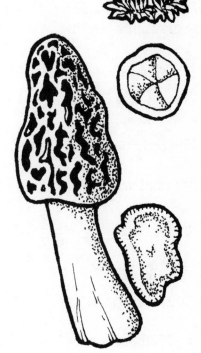

1. If slime mold grows on rotting logs, then circle B.
   If slime mold grows on desert sand, then circle C.

2. If fungi can grow as big as a rabbit, then circle A.
   If fungi can grow as big as a sheep, then circle R.

3. If the largest known fungus is in the state of Washington, then circle E.
   If the largest known fungus is in the state of California, then circle F.

4. If fungi cause measles, then circle M.
   If fungi cause athlete's foot, then circle A.

5. If fungi is a plant, then circle O.
   If fungi is an animal, then circle G.
   If fungi is its own category, then circle D.

6. If some mushrooms are poisonous, then circle O.
   If no mushrooms are poisonous, then circle D.

7. If mold can grow on cold mountain sites, then circle R.
   If mold can grow under the sea, then circle T.

8. If moss is a fungus, then circle H.
   If yeast is a fungus, then circle I.

9. If fungi caused the 1918 flu epidemic, then circle M.
   If fungi caused the 1840s potato famine, then circle S.

10. If mold was a source of aspirin, then circle Y.
    If mold was a source of penicillin, then circle E.

Puzzle: Fungi cause ___ ___ ___ ___ ___   T ___   ___ ___ ___ ___ .
                      1   2   3   4   5   6   7   8   9 10

Name _____

A Word Within Words

Directions: Each word below includes the word **but**. Can you identify each?

1. __ __ __ __ __ __ __ __ __ __ __   a meat cutter

2. __ __ __ __ __ __ __   an abruptly raised hill

3. __ __ __ __ __ __ __ __ __ __ __   a white walnut tree

4. __ __ __ __ __ __ __   a city in southwest Montana

5. __ __ __ __ __ __ __ __ __   an answer in defense

6. __ __ __ __ __ __ __ __   a spread for bread

7. __ __ __ __ __ __ __ __ __   a large flat fish

8. __ __ __ __ __ __   to join end to end

9. __ __ __ __ __ __ __ __   a garment fastener

10. __ __ __ __ __   to collide

11. __ __ __ __ __ __ __ __ __ __ __   a broad-winged insect

12. __ __ __ __ __ __ __   a first public appearance

13. __ __ __ __ __ __ __ __ __ __ __ __ __ __ __   a candy made from melted butter, brown sugar, and corn syrup

14. __ __ __ __ __ __ __   flammable gas made from petroleum or natural gas

15. __ __ __ __ __ __ __ __ __ __ __ __ __ __   a protein-rich spread used on sandwiches

16. __ __ __ __ __ __ __ __ __ __   a yellow or white flowered herb

17. __ __ __ __ __ __ __   a head servant

18. __ __ __ __ __ __ __ __ __   a supporting wall

Name _____

Ferdinand Magellan

Directions: Read the story and answer the questions which follow.

Ferdinand Magellan was a patriotic Portuguese soldier who had fought well for his country and King Manuel. So why was he siding with King Charles of Spain, Manuel's arch enemy?

In 1517 Manuel and Charles were the two most powerful rulers of the Western world. Both ruled over sea-trading empires, willing to colonize wherever riches could be amassed. In fact, in 1494 the Pope had stepped in to prevent an all-out war between the two neighboring superpowers. In the Treaty of Tordesillas, the two nations settled claims as to which had exploration rights in the Americas and the Far East.

But no one knew which nation could lay claim to the wealth of the Spice Islands. Were they Portuguese or Spanish? The trading prospects were certainly *enticing*, and so both countries wanted the islands.

The Portuguese, by treaty, could sail around the African continent to the Spice Islands. That was *their* right. They built many ports along the African coast to support their trade. So what could the Spanish do?

That was where Magellan stepped in. Rumor had it that this Portuguese noble had a huge fight with King Manuel. In anger, Magellan turned to King Charles of Spain with this suggestion: Sponsor a fleet of five ships, and Magellan would sail around the southern tip of the Americas (Spanish-held land), cross the South Sea (the Pacific Ocean), and prove that the Spice Islands are within Spanish territory. Charles agreed to this financial agreement. He could afford to provide the ships. Plus, he could then best his political rival, King Manuel.

So five ships were repaired and outfitted for this journey. Sailors were hired from throughout Europe. It was hard finding sailors daring enough for this crazy undertaking. Secrecy was maintained. The Spanish expedition might anger the Portuguese enough that they would halt the venture. Food supplies were gathered and stored. Trade goods were stashed. Finally in August of 1519, with a crew of 237 men, Magellan set sail.

There were a number of troubles. First, the ships had to travel through uncharted waters. The sailors had no records of wind direction, ocean current, or sea depths. With his men fearing the unknown, Magellan often had to stop mutinies—particularly among his nobles and captains. He had to hang some of the ringleaders.

Second, the Portuguese learned of the plan. They sent spies to *thwart* Magellan's mission and start rebellions. In later years, Magellan's friends suspected these spies of loading his ships with rotted food.

Third, hunger was a problem. Food supplies ran short during the three-year voyage. Magellan's projections for crossing the Pacific Ocean were far too optimistic. And when his crews were near land, they often had to stay away from the coastal towns that were controlled by the Portuguese. At times, the sailors ate sawdust, insects, mice, and leather.

Fourth, there were worms. Wooden ships were tasty food for some larvae. Over time these worms chewed through the old wooden ships, making them weak and prone to leaks.

Fifth, there were other enemies. Of course, the Spanish were on the lookout for Portuguese ships and avoided them whenever possible. But the biggest blow to the explorers came at a group of islands Magellan named *The Philippines* in honor of Prince Philip of Spain. The Spanish fleet befriended a local chieftain and his people whom they baptized into the Christian faith. By partnering with this tribe and defending it in battle, the Spanish made enemies with a vast and powerful army of warring people. Magellan and forty of his crew were killed before the remaining Spanish could escape with their lives.

Shipwrecked, starved, imprisoned, diseased, the large force of Spanish adventurers dwindled in number. Only one small ship with twenty-two men (four of whom were Spice Islanders) completed the journey. They returned to Seville, Spain, in September 1522.

Did the Spanish crown obtain big profit from the journey? They did not. Although the one returning ship was filled with 25 tons of cloves, that barely covered the cost of the trip. Did Spain keep the rights to the Spice Island claim? No, again. In 1527, King Charles sold the rights to Portugal for 350,000 golden ducats.

Magellan's survivors did prove for all time that humans could *circumnavigate* the earth. Plus, the ships' logs and journals advanced knowledge of the vast earth for people of the time, and for generations to come.

1. What did King Charles want? _____

2. Why did the Pope help design a treaty? _____
   _____

3. How did Magellan die? _____

4. Besides Magellan's death, what were five problems the Spanish fleet encountered? _____
   _____
   _____

5. What spice did Magellan's crew return with? _____

6. What does *enticing* mean?   revolutionary   attractive   deceptive   bold

7. What does *thwart* mean?   kill   organize   choose   stop

8. What is the meaning of the word *circumnavigate*?
   sail around   map   draw upon   destroy

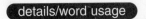
Sir Francis Drake, the "Sea Dog"

Directions: Read the story and answer the questions which follow.

In 1567 Francis Drake, John Hawkins, and other English seamen were on a voyage. They hoped to make a profit by selling smuggled goods to some of the Spanish colonies. On their way back from their voyage, they stopped at a Mexican port. While in port, Spanish ships, pretending at first to be friendly, attacked them. Drake and Hawkins barely escaped with their lives. The Spaniards killed many of their men and sank many of their ships. Undaunted, Drake continued to pursue a life at sea. Drake became a captain, military commander, buccaneer, and a "sea dog."

Drake and other English captains were called "sea dogs" during the rule of Queen Elizabeth I. They were supported and encouraged by the queen to loot, raid, and take all they could from the Spanish ships they encountered. Queen Elizabeth gave the "sea dogs" money and ships, and she also shared in their many profits. Drake, the most famous of these sea captains, was such a feared buccaneer, or pirate, that the Spanish called him "El Draque" or "The Dragon."

By far, Drake is best known as the first Englishman to sail around the world. At the start of this voyage, the three main ships in his party were the *Pelican*, the *Elizabeth*, and the *Marigold*. Two other ships transported supplies. While traveling Drake captured a Portuguese ship. He then lost some of his ships due to their poor conditions and others due to a storm, leaving only the *Marigold*, which was pushed far off course. Drake then renamed it the *Golden Hind*.

Traveling in the newly named *Golden Hind*, Drake raided several Spanish settlements. The settlements were not guarded because previously only Spanish ships had sailed there. Drake captured the Spanish ship, *Cacafuego*, and took all of its treasure. He then traveled up the coast of North America, eventually landing in what we know today as San Francisco and claimed the land for England. While there, he repaired his ship and decided to continue traveling around the world instead of going back the way he came. After circling the world, Drake returned to England a hero. The voyage had taken three years.

In 1581, Queen Elizabeth knighted Drake, Sir Francis Drake. His voyage had opened the doors for the British in the Pacific Ocean and helped to increase trading in eastern Asia. He also brought much knowledge of travel and of the world that helped future explorers.

Drake took his last voyage in 1595 with John Hawkins. Sir Francis Drake died off the coast of Panama and was buried at sea by his crew.

1. Who is Sir Francis Drake? _____

2. What role did the Queen play with the "sea dogs"? _____

3. What is a *buccaneer*? _____

4. Who was a "sea dog"? _____

5. List five facts about Sir Francis Drake and his travels.

   a. _____

   b. _____

   c. _____

   d. _____

   e. _____

6. Match these words with their descriptions.

   _____ San Francisco   a. Spanish treasure ship

   _____ Mexican port   b. Spanish word for "The Dragon"

   _____ John Hawkins   c. Where Drake stopped to repair his ship

   _____ *Golden Hind*   d. Where Spanish attacked Drake and Hawkins

   _____ *Cacafuego*   e. Seaman who traveled with Drake

   _____ "El Draque"   f. Drake's ship

7. After repairing his ship, why do you think Drake decided to continue traveling around the world instead of going back the way he came?

   _____

8. Why did Queen Elizabeth knight Drake in 1581?

   _____

   _____

9. The voyage Drake was most well-known for was...

   a. traveling to the Spanish colonies with John Hawkins in 1567.
   b. traveling to the Mexican port and being attacked by the Spanish.
   c. traveling around the world in the ship he renamed the *Golden Hind*.
   d. traveling along the coast of Panama in 1595 just before his death.

10. Why do you think Drake renamed his ship the *Golden Hind?*

   _____

   _____

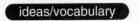

Name _____

Lights, Camera, Action!

Directions: Read the selections and answer the questions which follow.

Below are three reports. Each is to be read aloud to a class while computer-generated pictures share the information visually.

1. How would you travel over water in Ancient Egypt? Believe it or not, you would float on paper. In 3000 B.C., the early Egyptian boats were constructed from the *papyrus* plant. These reeds, from which early paper was made, could grow to be 20 feet high. The reeds were cut and bundled and tied tightly together. Bundles were lashed together, and their ends—which became the bow and stern of the boat—would be pulled to curve upward. The stern, or back, was shaped so it rose high above the water. Then the stern's reedy end would be curved into a comma shape. Even when the Egyptians started using wood, they shaped their watercraft like this.

2. What job might you have aboard a ship if you live in 2500 B.C.? In Egypt, you might have worked on a sailing ship. With the Egyptians' limited knowledge of navigation, they could only sail with the wind. A steady breeze blew south and up the Nile River all year long. If you had worked on one of these ships, you may have served as a *helmsman*. Six quick-witted guides stood at the stern of the ship. Each one held a large oar, and the six oars acted as a rudder to change the ship's course. Other jobs included cooking the food and protecting the cargo. Another sailor would be given the job of pouring water on the heavy central rope to keep the ship strong. But the most back-breaking work was the job of *oarsman*, to row whenever your ship came into port or ventured downstream.

3. We have a description of a typical Egyptian trade journey, which was found on the walls of Queen Hatshepsut's burial temple. The journey took the ship south through the Red Sea to the lands of present-day Ethiopia and Somalia. Before sailing, the crew made a sacrifice to the goddess Hathor, to ask for a wind that blew in the right direction. They had a huge sail on the ship, thirty oarsmen, and many articles of trade. When the ship arrived in the land called Punt, the sailors were greeted by the chief and his people. The Egyptians offered to trade them bread, wine, dried fruits, honey cakes, necklaces, daggers, and axes. The people of Punt had exotic treasures: wild leopards, ivory, apes, ebony, and thirty-one scented *myrrh* trees, which were used to make incense and for embalming. Queen Hathshepsut, the only known female pharoah, had the trees planted on the grounds of her temple.

1. Write phrases to describe these terms from the articles.

a. papyrus _____

b. early sails _____

c. helmsman _____

d. Punt _____

e. Hatshepsut _____

2. Circle the central theme of each of the reports.

Report 1	**ship jobs**	**Egypt**	**ship construction**	**temple**	**trade**
Report 2	**ship jobs**	**Egypt**	**ship construction**	**temple**	**trade**
Report 3	**ship jobs**	**Egypt**	**ship construction**	**temple**	**trade**

3. Write the word from the articles whose definitions are listed here.

Report 1   **clusters tied together** _____

                back of ship _____

                rest on the water _____

Report 2   **someone who rows** _____

                steering device on ship _____

                goods carried on ship _____

Report 3   **an offering to the gods** _____

                an aromatic plant _____

                strange or unusual _____

Name _____

Amazing Animals

Directions: Match each animal with its special feature correctly and you will solve the puzzle below. Use reference materials when you need help.

Can you tell what is so special about these creatures?

_____	1. bumblebee bat	B	fastest animal in the world
_____	2. box turtle	D	heaviest snake
_____	3. pigeon	A	can stay in the air for months without rest
_____	4. albatross	O	spends most of its life upside down
_____	5. Russian sturgeon	E	ate stones because it did not chew well
_____	6. swift	L	a group of this is called a *down*
_____	7. hare	P	may live to be 100 years old
_____	8. chimpanzee	O	simplest animal form
_____	9. sloth	F	belongs to the animal group annelids
_____	10. anaconda	M	a fish with the largest eggs
_____	11. earthworm	E	can produce 188 decibels of sound
_____	12. giant squid	S	the smallest mammal
_____	13. protozoa	R	has the largest eyes of all animals
_____	14. whale shark	Y	the only bird known to attack and kill humans
_____	15. fin whale	O	besides humans, the best maker of tools
_____	16. ostrich	R	its young is called a *squab*
_____	17. sauropod	Y	produces caviar, an expensive food

The Texas Horned Lizard, when picked up by humans, may puff itself up and do this.

___ ___ ___ ___ ___   ___ ___ ___ ___ ___   ___ ___ ___ ___ corners of its ___ ___ ___s
 1   2   3   4   5   6   7   8   9 10   11 12 13 14   15 16 17

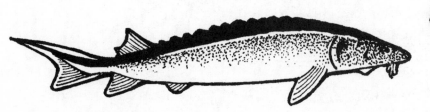

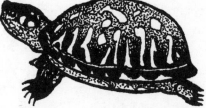

69   0-7424-0220-7 *Nonfiction Reading Comprehension*

Name _____

Awesome Sites

Directions: Read the story and answer the questions which follow.

Cave of Ten Thousand Buddhas

Along the banks of the River Yishui in eastern China is a series of cave temples. These caves, known to us as the Longman Caves, are dedicated to the Buddha, a prince from India. Some of these cave temples were first carved out and established in A.D. 494, but the Cave of Ten Thousand Buddhas, or *Wanfo dong*, was opened in A.D. 680.

The cave room itself is a large square. Its side walls are covered with thousands of small images of Buddha, carved into the walls. This is known as *bas-relief*. Besides the tiny figures are a large Buddha and four of his followers on the front wall. Many images of musicians also adorn the chamber.

The making of such limestone carving art at the caves ended more than 1,000 years ago. Still, visitors travel to the site to see this beautiful architecture.

Krak des Chevaliers

In Syria a major conflict arose between two hostile groups. For centuries Christians traveled through the region to visit the Holy Land and to follow a major trade route to the Far East. Muslim Arabs had made Syria their empire center. But another, fairly vigorous people, the Turks, took over the region. After they had adopted the Muslim faith, they came to quarrel with Christian pilgrims. This conflict became known to European Christians as the Crusades.

A Muslim stronghold along the trade route to the Far East was attacked by crusading knights. They converted the fortress into a massive, seemingly impregnable structure which they renamed "the castle of the knights" or *Krak des Chevaliers*.

This massive structure could house 2,000 soldiers and their horses, a five-year supply of food, and all the knights' fighting equipment. It had a maze of rooms, passages, chapels, and large halls. It had an aqueduct to supply fresh water, a series of gates and walls to hold off attacking enemies, and 13 towers.

The fortress has survived. The Christian defenders did not. After 130 years of occupation and after a month-long battle in 1271, the crusaders were fooled into surrender.

Tenochtitlán

How does one choose where to settle down? According to legend, the Aztec sun god, Huitzilopochtli, told his people to settle where an eagle, perched on a cactus, held a snake in its talons. In 1325 this band of wandering hunters found the sign. They built their village on a marshy island in central Mexico.

The village expanded quickly. The Aztecs created land by dredging mud from their shallow lake and by constructing floating islands made of reed platforms.

Tenochtitlán, the place of the prickly pear cactus, developed into a city of islands which were connected by canals and raised paths. By 1500 it held a massive pyramid upon which two temples rested. One temple was reserved for the sun god, the other for the rain god Tlaloc. This former village at the time was probably the largest city in the world.

It did not last. The Spanish soldiers who came destroyed the city and its buildings, bringing an end to the Aztec empire. But today we can travel to Mexico City, built on the ruins of the wondrous ancient city.

1. Name the building or structure which came from these places:

   Mexico _____

   China _____

   Syria _____

2. What was the purpose of each structure?

   Cave of 10,000 Buddhas _____

   Krak des Chevaliers _____

   Tenochtitlán _____

3. What is meant by the following:

   bas-relief _____

   Huitzilopochtli _____

   crusades _____

   Buddha _____

   reed platforms _____

   castle of the knights _____

4. Which of these structures can we still visit today?

   _____

   _____

Name _____

On the Fly

Directions: Match pairs of synonyms by writing the correct word in the blank. Fill in the numbered blanks below with the letters next to each synonym. Use a dictionary for help.

_____ 1. highborn	race	O
_____ 2. vigorous	gulp	M
_____ 3. keen	flounder	S
_____ 4. gobble	ecstasy	E
_____ 5. latch	secure	U
_____ 6. trinket	gleeful	G
_____ 7. luxurious	insignia	E
_____ 8. lark	swivel	N
_____ 9. bliss	royal	O
_____ 10. placid	saturate	T
_____ 11. wail	serene	S
_____ 12. expire	storm	N
_____ 13. badge	stationery	N
_____ 14. squall	strenuous	U
_____ 15. vessel	theme	O
_____ 16. huddle	trifle	S
_____ 17. blunder	quiver	U
_____ 18. drench	container	O
_____ 19. colorful	vivid	R
_____ 20. dart	sob	A
_____ 21. notepaper	wilt	G
_____ 22. droop	bunch	T
_____ 23. nucleus	perceptive	R
_____ 24. pivot	adventure	L
_____ 25. premise	elegant	C
_____ 26. twitch	core	E
_____ 27. jovial	shelter	H
_____ 28. haven	cease	R

Why can't we fly with da Vinci's wing design?

__ __ __ __ __ __ __ __ __ __ __ __ __ __ __ __
1 2 3   4 5 6 7   8 9 10   11 12 13   14 15 16

__ __ __ __ __ __ __ __ __ __ __ __ __.
17 18 19 20 21 22 23 24 25 26 27 28

Name _____

Don't Mind If I Do

Directions: Match the two parts of each statement below.

Part 1

_____ 1. Eight bones of your skull make up the braincase or cranium . . .

_____ 2. Because nerves are not connected with each other, . . .

_____ 3. If your brain does not get enough oxygen, . . .

_____ 4. If a leg nerve is pinched and cannot transfer messages, . . .

_____ 5. Glial cells, which outnumber neurons in the brain ten to one, attack invading bacteria . . .

_____ 6. Because the brain feels no pain, . . .

_____ 7. The human brain lies within a liquid solution . . .

_____ 8. Because the sense of taste is related to the sense of smell, . . .

_____ 9. Because our memories are not always reliable, . . .

_____ 10. Because each second millions of signals pass through our brains, . . .

_____ 11. Because girls' left brains often develop earlier, . . .

_____ 12. Because signals in your skin travel along up to 400 feet per second, . . .

_____ 13. The central nerve, or spinal cord, rests . . .

_____ 14. If a person is not permitted to sleep, . . .

Part 2

a. we are able to think.

b. to keep us healthy.

c. a message must leap from one to the other.

d. you react quickly to heat or pain.

e. to form a hard protection for your brain.

f. to protect and cushion it from shock.

g. within the human spine, made up of 33 separate vertebrae.

h. you will feel dizzy and you may lose consciousness.

i. when you have a stuffy nose, food may taste unexciting to you.

j. we unconsciously change or make up ideas that we add to our real memory.

k. he may begin to see or hear things that are not there.

l. a brain surgeon can work on a fully awake patient.

m. they may develop better speaking skills.

n. your leg may go to sleep temporarily.

Challenge: Try to recall everything you can from an experience you had four days ago with one or more others. Each of you should jot down your memories on paper. Do you agree? Do you have different memories?

Name _____

To Be or Not to Be

Directions: Read the story and answer the questions which follow.

The whooping crane, the tallest bird of North America, is in danger of extinction. Hunted down by hunters, its wetland habitat often destroyed by builders, the number of these graceful birds went to about 600 by 1870. Further hunting and land development reduced the crane population to only sixteen by 1940. But concerned people have stepped in. Additional bird refuges or *sanctuaries* have been established along the two thousand miles of flyway, so cranes can rest as they move from their summer to winter homes. A program for captive breeding was started in 1967 to increase the number of cranes. Normally, female whooping cranes lay two eggs per year, only one of which hatches. Naturalists search for the nests and remove one egg from each. These "birdnapped" babies are hatched and reared by hand. The number of whooping cranes has not risen quickly. First, the bird does not mate until it is five years old. Second, disease sometimes kills the captive birds. Third, less than half of all rescued eggs produce cranes that reach adulthood. A flock was established in 1974 by placing whooping crane eggs in the nests of the smaller sandhill crane. It worked! The whooping crane is returning.

Write down the effect which follows each cause below.

1. As the crane lost its marshland habitat, _____

2. Because only one egg matures in the whooping crane's nest, _____
   _____

3. Because a large distance separates the summer and winter homes of the crane,
   _____

4. Since the bird does not mate until it is five years old, _____
   _____

5. Sandhill cranes serve as parents, _____

6. When hunting continued between 1870 and 1940, _____
   _____
   _____

74

Name _____

Achievements and Discoveries

Directions: Read the material and fill in the grid to discover the rest of the information..

Naomi, a sixth-grade student, took many notes at the meeting for Achievement Studies at City High. She is not well organized. Use her six note cards to match the five explorers, including Cousteau, with their year of exploration, their achievement, and their cultural background.

Card 1: Neither the Arab nor Gagarin, who was not the 1900 explorer, invented the Aqua-Lung.

Card 2: Hedin lived before the Aqua-Lung inventor but after the man who crossed the Sahara. Coronado, second of these explorers, was at least two explorers before the orbiter.

Card 3: In order of achievement from early to late are Hedin, the Aqua-Lung inventor, and Gagarin, who is not Spanish.

Card 4: Ibn Battuta, an Arab, was one of the two earliest explorers.

Card 5: The explorer of the Grand Canyon lived before the French explorer (who had not crossed the Sahara), who did not have the 1961 achievement. The Swede did his work in 1900.

Card 6: The 1540 Spanish explorer found the Grand Canyon . . . well, Native Americans already knew about it.

		Year					Achievement					Culture				
		1350	1540	1900	1943	1961	IA	MCA	DGC	OE	CS	A	F	So	Sp	Sw
Explorer	Battuta															
	Coronado															
	Cousteau															
	Gagarin															
	Hedin															
Culture	Arab															
	French															
	Soviet															
	Spanish															
	Swedish															
Achievement	invented Aqua-Lung															
	mapped Central Asia															
	discovered Grand Canyon															
	orbited Earth															
	crossed Sahara															

Name _____

Getting Out of Danger

Directions: Match each animal to its native land and to a chief cause for its return.

Environmentalists are having some success. In recent years these five animals have shown signs of "coming back."

1. The Canadian animal who is not the tortoise either had a park created for it or tourism established to increase its numbers. Two of the animals were helped by United States causes.

2. The tortoise, the Wyoming animal, and the park-aided creature are all North American.

3. Tourism has helped either the Indonesian creature or the tamarin.

4. The creature from Brazil, not the beluga, was aided through captive breeding. It has now been reintroduced to its rainforest home.

5. The Komodo dragon is not from Brazil or Canada.

6. The pronghorn antelope, who caused the demise of the motorcycle race, is an animal whose benefit also came in the United States.

	Location					Activity				
	Brazil	Canada	Indon.	Mohave	WY	cb	ep	rf	smr	t
beluga										
desert tortoise										
golden lion tamarin										
Komodo dragon										
pronghorn										
captive breeding										
established park										
removed fence										
stopped motorcycle race										
tourism										

Animal

Activity

Name _____

The Wright Stuff

Directions: Read the story and answer the questions which follow.

What is the background of the Wright brothers? First, Wilbur, born in Millville, Indiana, in 1867, is older by four years. Second, Orville, born in Dayton, Ohio, was, like his brother, curious, mathematically gifted, and inquisitive. Their father was a minister and editor; their mother was able to repair just about anything around the house. The boys, who always enjoyed machines, grew increasingly interested in mechanics. They began their own four-page Dayton newspaper which competed with the larger local dailies for four months. Next they turned to bicycle work. Their business thrived when the Wright Special, a bicycle which sold for $18, made the Wright Cycle Company a successful business.

How did they turn to airplanes? The young men had been moved by the death of a German inventor, Otto Lilienthal. This man had built and flown glider planes in Europe and had received much publicity. His death resulted from a failed flight. Both Wright brothers felt that someone should continue Lilienthal's ideas. Why not them? So they tinkered and experimented. They built kites and gliders, wind tunnels, and wing types. They designed rudders and engines. Then they tested their products over sand dunes and pastures. They took lots of notes. Wilbur was the first to try powered flight. When he pulled too hard on the plane's elevator, the Flyer came crashing down. So it was younger brother Orville, three days later (after the two had repaired the battered machine), who was sent skyward on the historic first flight of December 17, 1903.

Were they an immediate success? The two mechanics and inventors continued to improve their machines. Without a patent, they were unwilling to let others photograph their work. They feared that others would claim the invention. Most Americans scoffed at their claims of success. The U.S. War Department did not even accept offers to have the aircraft demonstrated for them. Only after French businessmen made business offers to the brothers did the U.S. government change its mind. By 1908, it was clear that aviation was changing the world.

1. Who is the older brother? _____

2. What two other businesses did the brothers have? _____

3. What is the Wright Special? _____

4. Where would the inventors practice flying their gliders and early planes?

   _____

5. Which brother took the first flight? _____

6. Describe the brothers' skills using four adjectives. _____

   _____

7. Why wouldn't the world believe the Wrights for many years? _____

Name _____

Another Moses?

Directions: Match the secondary information sentences to one of these four headings.

Clara Brown was born a slave. In 1856, she was able to buy her freedom. In later years, she helped many other former slaves succeed in life. But life was tough. Match the secondary information sentences to one of these four major headings.

A. **Go West**: 1859 Brown leaves her home in Missouri to make a new life.
B. **Making a Living**: 1859–1866 Brown continues to work hard in Colorado to survive and prosper.
C. **Aunt Clara Brown**: 1866–1881 Having no success finding her daughter, Brown helps others find work.
D. **Her Mission**: 1856–1883 Ever since freedom came, Brown tried to find her daughter.

_____ 1. She had to prove to fellow travelers that she was not a slave.

_____ 2. She bought seven houses by saving her earnings.

_____ 3. She traveled to many towns searching for information.

_____ 4. With other former slaves, she returned by wagon to her home out west.

_____ 5. She taught others how to begin businesses.

_____ 6. A friend told Clara about a woman who might be her daughter.

_____ 7. She could make fifty cents for each shirt she washed.

_____ 8. She had to walk 680 miles to reach Colorado.

_____ 9. She settled in Central City, Colorado.

_____ 10. She found many former slaves displaced following the Civil War.

_____ 11. She wrote to friends to try to get news of her daughter Eliza.

_____ 12. She asked a travel party if she might join them.

_____ 13. She set up a laundry service in the mining town.

_____ 14. Her many friends wrote to newspapers so Clara could receive a pension.

_____ 15. She traveled to Iowa, hoping for a miracle.

_____ 16. She was not permitted to ride or sleep in the wagons on her journey west.

_____ 17. She paid for safe travel for twenty-six former slaves.

_____ 18. She cooked for others on the trail.

_____ 19. She recognized her daughter.

_____ 20. She gave everyone a home or land.

_____ 21. Along the rough road, she nursed sick fellow travelers.

_____ 22. She rode to Kentucky where her daughter had been born.

_____ 23. She succeeded in owning $10,000 in land and cash.

Name _____

Birthday Doubles

Directions: Using clues below and other resources, match the people to their birthdays.

1. **January 1**   a silversmith patriot and the FBI director

   _____   _____   1735   1895

2. **January 27**   creator of Alice and a classical composer

   _____   _____   1832   1756

3. **February 12**   *Fudge* author and author of the Gettysburg Address

   _____   _____   1938   1809

4. **April 21**   a royal ruler and *Who's the Boss* star?

   _____   _____   1926   1951

5. **May 29**   famous patriot and entertainer of the troops

   _____   _____   1736   1903

6. **June 12**   U.S. President and war-diary writer

   _____   _____   1924   1929

7. **July 12**   ice-skater and TV star/comedian

   _____   _____   1971   1937

8. **July 24**   woman aviator and Latin freedom fighter

   _____   _____   1897   1783

9. **October 2**   nonviolent revolutionary and famous comedian brother

   _____   _____   1869   1890

10. **November 29**   authors of *Little Women* and *A Wrinkle in Time*

    _____   _____   1832   1918

11. **November 30**   Gulliver's and Huck's creators

    _____   _____   1667   1835

12. **December 30**   leading golfer and Dodger southpaw

    _____   _____   1975   1935

Louisa May Alcott	Anne Frank	Judy Blume	Mahatma Gandhi
Abraham Lincoln	Simón Bolívar	Mia Hamm	Groucho Marx
Madeleine L'Engle	Patrick Henry	Lewis Carroll	George Bush
J. Edgar Hoover	Paul Revere	Bob Hope	Bill Cosby
Jonathan Swift	Mark Twain	Amelia Earhart	
Wolfgang Mozart	Tiger Woods	Kristi Yamaguchi	
Queen Elizabeth II	Sandy Koufax	Tony Danza	

Name _____

Julius Caesar

Directions: Read the selection and answer the questions that follow.

He came, he saw, and he conquered. To whom does this famous quote refer? To Julius Caesar, the famous Roman emperor.

Julius was born in 100 B.C., the son of Gaius Caesar. He came from a *patrician* family. Patricians were the nobles, rich and powerful Romans. Patrician senators were the men who could present laws to the Roman republic. Julius's family, the Julii, claimed to be descendants of the goddess Venus.

Julius was ambitious. When he was very young, his parents nominated him to be a priest of Jupiter, the chief of the Roman gods. As a priest, Julius had contact with many important people. He married the daughter of a powerful leader. Julius and his friends were called the *populares* because they tried to please the poorest people of the city. To become popular with more people, Julius trained to become a gifted speaker. A quick learner, and eager for attention, he also trained as a soldier. Soon, others noticed his military talent, and he was given soldiers to lead into battle. Every time his army won a victory, Julius broadcast his success so that the Romans back home heard about it. To further spread his name and fame, Julius Caesar wrote a book about his victories.

By persuading other aristocrats, by planning elaborate social events like the gladiator fights and a mock naval battle in the Colosseum, Julius had himself elected to many important offices. While this frightened or angered many of his fellow Roman aristocrats, it pleased the masses of Roman citizens. Julius also won battles in lands that are today's Germany, France, Spain, Egypt, Turkey, England, Italy, and Greece. After so much success, he was elected Roman dictator for ten years. That was a first; up to that time dictators were elected for only six months in times of emergency, such as war. Now Julius was convinced of his popularity. Sometimes the Romans offered an official celebration called a triumph. These were given to celebrate and honor a general's victory over his enemies.

Julius Caesar had always been brave. When still a young man, he was kidnapped by Mediterranean pirates. Stomping boldly across the open deck of his "prison," Julius pointed out the pirates' mistakes. Furthermore, he announced to his captors that he could and would defeat them! They laughed. When Julius's ransom was paid and he was freed, he kept his word. He captured the pirates and had them put to death.

Julius continued to reach for more power. He was willing to anger other aristocrats to get his way. After all, he was very popular with the poor. But he went too far. The Romans elected him dictator for life, and he accepted this offer. In March of 44 B.C., a group of rich senators, fearing that their power had been stolen, surrounded him and stabbed him to death. Among them were Julius's close friends. Their fears were justified. The Roman Senate never had its power returned. New dictators took over. And from this man's death until the end of the Roman Empire, each new emperor took *Caesar* as a title.

1. Name five things Julius did to become popular.

   _____   _____

   _____   _____

   _____

2. Circle the word that is a synonym for *patrician*.

   smart   wise   noble   brave

3. Who were the *populares*? _____

   _____

4. Before Julius Caesar, when might the Romans elect a dictator? _____

   _____

5. What was a *triumph*? _____

   _____

6. Circle the adjectives which describe Roman senators.

   poor   male   foreign   soldiers   law-making   wealthy

7. How had Julius Caesar frightened the senators?_____

   _____

8. Which adjective describes Caesar's attitude toward the pirates?

   silent   frightened   admiring   brave

Name _____

Hitch Your Wagon to a Star

Directions: Complete the chart to match each idiom with its meaning and an example.

Idiom	Meaning	Example
1. go over like a lead balloon		
2.		one might lock one's diary
3.	to become fond of	
4. lower the boom		
5.	just what is expected	
6. on the ball		
7.	to be greatly inferior	

Idioms:
take a shine to
par for the course
mum's the word
can't hold a candle to

Meanings:
to punish severely
skillful and alert
a boss
fail miserably
tell no one the secret
to remain calm

Examples:
young girl for her new kitten
George W. Bush
fireworks on Independence Day
what one would hope of a pilot
an attempt to be perfect for a day
hot dog to T-bone
Aunt Polly when she found out Tom had gone swimming

Name _____

Up Above My Head

Directions: Read the story and answer the questions which follow.

When you look up at the sky on a clear night, what do you see? Can you see the planets and stars, or is your vision obscured by city lights, buildings, or air pollution? If you could see into the night sky clearly, you might be surprised by what's up there . . . or by what's beyond your vision.

For example, in early 2001, the earth launched an amazing plan for an international space station, or *ISS*. Since it was begun in 1998, much of the station is in orbit 250 miles above us. A trio of scientists made up the station's Expedition One crew. When the station is completed in 2006, it will house an international village in its "two-football-field-sized" maze of laboratory modules, power plants, and living spaces. A total of forty-six space missions are needed to send up the parts of the *ISS* construction. Already astronomers are telling us that *ISS* may appear as bright as Sirius or even Venus.

Sometimes space missions run very well. In 1989, NASA launched *Galileo*, a relatively small probe, to examine Jupiter and its satellites or moons. The *Galileo* not only completed its planned two-year mission, but it has also executed an additional two-year study of Europa, one of Jupiter's moons. Because *Galileo* is still fully functional, it is now on its way to yet another Jovian moon, Io. Should scientists consider further plans for this probe that just won't quit?

Did you ever hear of the first Lagrangian point? It is the place in space between the Earth and the sun where the gravitational pull of the two large spheres exert an equal force. In 1995, four of Earth's agencies sponsored the launching of *SOHO* to check out the sun's activities. The *Solar and Heliospheric Observatory* is locked in at the first Lagrangian point where nothing can get in its line of vision with the sun. It even allows scientists to see below the surface of the sun.

Earth already has a probe checking out the 20-mile-long asteroid called Eros. The *NEAR* probe (*Near Earth Asteroid Rendezvous*) was launched in 1996 and is scheduled to ditch on the asteroid's surface February 2002. It has already taken more than 160,000 pictures of that large space rock.

But we have other probes in the works. One, named *Deep Impact*, is scheduled for its terrestrial departure in 2004. It will meet up with Comet P/Tempel 1. Actually, it should slam deep into the comet's interior in mid-2005 and send back to Earth data which will disclose the composition of this space snowball.

Will we send space scientists to places beyond *ISS*? Perhaps. Let's hope that no one experiences what Sergei Krikalev's did. In May of 1991 he was sent to the old space station, *Mir*. His plans were to remain in space for five months. But while he was completing his tasks on *Mir*, his country of Russia underwent a period of civil unrest. Russia's space program was "put on hold." Krikalev was stranded in space. Eventually he was picked up and returned to Earth—five months later than his scheduled recovery!

The sky is a fascinating place and outer space is an endless place for exploration.

1. List the year launched and the mission of each of these programs.

	Year Launched	Mission
a. ISS	_____	_____
b. NEAR	_____	_____
c. SOHO	_____	_____
d. Galileo	_____	_____

2. What is the First Lagrangian point? _____
_____

3. Why was Krikalev stuck in space? _____
_____

4. Which probe plans to smash into a comet? _____
_____

5. Debate Question: What benefits do space probes like these have for humans?
_____
_____
_____
_____

Name _____

Famous People

Directions: Match each fact about the famous person or people with their names to the left.

1. Amelia Earhart _____

2. The Inca _____

3. Vikings _____

4. Harry Houdini _____

5. Phillis Wheatly _____

6. Wang Yani _____

7. Julius Caesar _____

8. Florence Nightingale _____

9. Benjamin Franklin _____

10. Sir Francis Drake _____

a. American magician who could escape from many difficult situations such as chains, jail cells, and handcuffs.

b. Roman dictator, soldier, and statesman.

c. American inventor, ambassador, scientist, and public leader who was born in Boston.

d. Chinese artist who began painting at a very young age.

e. Indian people of South America who, at one time, ruled one of the largest and richest empires in the Americas.

f. Famous American aviator who disappeared while flying over the Pacific ocean.

g. English sea captain best known for his sail around the world.

h. Fearless sailors and adventurers who lived in Scandinavia.

i. Colonial poet who was a freed slave.

j. Reformer of hospital care and service provider during the Crimean War.

Name _____

The Lady with the Lamp

Directions: Read the story and answer the questions which follow.

In Great Britain 150 years ago, hospitals for the sick were unpleasant places. The surgeons would be found wearing blood- and grime-splattered clothing. They might refuse to change clothing or equipment between surgeries. Diseases traveled readily between patients in a filthy atmosphere where bedding and clothing frequently went unwashed. Hospital food was a meager benefit, sometimes tainted and thinly nourishing at best. Those who provided nursing care had little or no training and lacked motivation. The wealthy in this period did not send their family members to the hospital, but had doctors and nurses come to their homes.

But a young gentlewoman, trained and educated by her family and expected to enter society, surprised her loved ones when she was called to serve the sick in hospitals. Her family was shocked. They thought she should marry and raise a family. But Florence Nightingale did not follow her family's expectations. Instead, she left her home in England to train in Germany as a nurse. There were no adequate training facilities in England. Upon her return to England, she found work at the Institute for the Care of Sick Gentlewomen in the city of London. The work paid nothing; the conditions were horrific; her sister and her mother were scandalized. How could she do such menial work? But Florence changed the conditions at the hospital. Patients were given bells to ring so that nurses could give them assistance; a hot-water system was ordered and installed; newly recruited nurses were carefully screened and trained; a *dumb waiter* (a food-service elevator) was constructed so that warm food could be served promptly; and money-saving programs were introduced to the institute.

Yet only a handful of important people recognized Florence Nightingale's talents. Then a terrible war came to Eastern Europe. France, Turkey, and England united to declare war on Russia in 1854. Soldiers went off to the Crimean peninsula, north of the Black Sea. There they fought the Russian troops of the Tsar. In those days, army hospital conditions were much worse than what was found in regular hospitals. Many men became ill with disease, and often a stay in the hospital made things worse. When British citizens read about these problems in the newspapers, they complained loudly. Florence Nightingale was asked to work in a Turkish hospital where British soldiers received treatment.

Florence took thirty-eight women with her. They found a filthy army barracks, a camp with no furniture, open sewers, and no cooking facility. Immediately, the team set to work. They requested more medicine, blankets, socks, and toothbrushes from Britain. They painted the walls. They organized a laundry. They organized a kitchen and hired a cook who understood nutrition. Much of this was due to Florence's guidance and direction. She worked endlessly to prepare medical reports, sit with the dying, write letters for those unable, and improve hospital conditions. Every night Florence Nightingale walked the corridors of this Turkish hospital, roughly four miles of hallways, carrying her lantern. By the time she returned to England in 1856, all of the country knew of her labor.

For the rest of her life, Florence Nightingale worked for the sick, for better nursing training, and for disease prevention. She established a nurse training school. She wrote a book about nursing and another about hospital design. She pushed for medical reform in India, at that time part of the British Empire. She completed a three-year study of mothers and newborn children.

This amazing servant to the world fought the medical problems of her society to create nursing as a profession.

Correct these false statements:

1. Florence Nightingale was a French peasant. _____

_____

2. Her family approved of her interest in nursing. _____

3. One hundred fifty years ago English hospitals were clean, well-staffed institutions. _____

4. Florence went to Germany to train as an aviator. _____

5. One change she brought was the purchase of bells to call cows home. _____

_____

6. The wealthy always sent their sick to the hospitals. _____

7. Florence worked as a maid in a hospital in Russia. _____

8. While serving for two years in the army hospital, Florence walked 14 miles every morning. _____

Identify these terms:

9. dumb waiter _____

10. Crimean War _____

11. book writing _____

12. news correspondent _____

Name _____

What Is Power?

Directions: Read the story and answer the questions which follow.

Long ago, more than 3,000 years ago, a baby was born into the house of Aye, the Egyptian king's chief scribe and Grand Vizier. Her name was Nefertiti, "the beautiful one has come." As a child she often played with Prince Amenhotep, the son of the Egyptian king. The prince himself became king at the age of 13, when his father stepped down from the throne. Three years later Amenhotep married Nefertiti. She was only 15.

Though only a young man, Amenhotep was interested in knowledge. He placed smart counselors by his side to help rule the land. He engaged, or employed, Aye as his Grand Vizier, or prime minister. While his father was alive, Amenhotep sought out his counsel in governing the land. But the young king questioned the Egyptian religion.

The Egyptians believed in many gods. Chief among these gods at the time was Amon, the sun god. There were many priests of Amon, and they were powerful and persuasive. As he studied and pondered his beliefs, Amenhotep reached the conclusion that there was only one true god. His name was Aton, meaning "the sun." Readily the king's wife Nefertiti agreed to follow the king in his new-found faith. When Amenhotep ("Amon is satisfied") changed his name to Akhenaton ("he who is beneficial to Aton"), the king infuriated the priests of the sun god. Oblivious to the hatred he had purchased, Akhenaton established a new imperial city. Thebes, the old capital, had much of the old religion. The new city—the first totally planned city in the world—would be dedicated to Aton. Located down river from Thebes, it would bear the name Akhetaton. It would be two miles long and one-half-mile wide. It would be filled with temple, gardens, palaces, and beautiful art.

The young king, though an intelligent dreamer, was no match for the priests of Amon. The provoked priests stirred up the people, gained influence with the Egyptian army, and further weakened the throne. Akhenaton, saddened by the controversies facing his new religion and disappointed that he had no male heir, became ill and died at the age of 32. Queen Nefertiti placed a young boy—Tutankhaton—on the throne. Her youngest daughter was made his wife. Her father, Aye, became Grand Vizier once more. When King Tut, for that is the same boy, changed his name to Tutankhamon in order to revere Amon, the sun god, the old Egyptian religion returned in vigor and with retribution.

Little more is known of King Akhenaton and Queen Nefertiti. But in 1912 a team of archaeologists discovered the workroom of Tuthmose, a royal craftsman and sculptor of the time. In the chamber they unearthed a beautifully sculpted stone, the head of Queen Nefertiti.

Identify these:

1. "Amon is satisfied" _____

2. chief scribe to the king _____

3. sun god _____

4. Thebes _____

5. Akhenaton _____

6. Tuthmose _____

Answer these questions:

7. What does it mean that Aye was engaged? _____

8. Select a synonym for the word sought. _____

9. Did King Akhenaton have any sons? _____

10. Why did Akhenaton become a weak king? _____
_____

11. Thought question: For what reason do people want power? To what end should any one person be permitted to have power over others? May we ever choose to disregard the power granted to another? _____

_____

_____

_____

Name _____

Feel the Force

Directions: Fill in each blank with the correct word. Use a dictionary if you need help.

What is a force? It is anything that changes or tends to change the state of rest or the state of motion in an object.

1. A *laser* is a device that a. _____ a very strong beam of
   b. _____ with only one wave length.
      a. bites, wrecks, produces, walks   b. iron, light, cocoa, wood

2. A *sonic boom* is a loud noise produced by the c. _____ expansion of air
   molecules when an object d. _____ the speed of sound.
      c. rapid, steady, humid, body's   d. rotates, contains, loses, exceeds

3. A *fossil fuel* is any substance, such as oil, coal, or e. _____gas, made by
   the decay of organic f. _____
      e. blue, stationary, Marti, natural   f. trees, matter, water, snails

4. *Torque* is any g. _____ that acts to h. _____an object.
      g. pie, force, rush, fro   h. keep, buy, drop, turn

5. The *boiling point* is the i. _____ at which a substance changes from
   j. _____ to vapor.
      i. number line, humidity,
         temperature, volume   j. matter, liquid, state, solid

6. *Solar power* is the process of k. _____ electricity from the
   l. _____.
      k. buying, generating, heating, wasting   l. planet, moon, sun, comet

7. An *airfoil* is any object, such as an airplane wing, m. _____ to cause
   lift when n. _____ through the air.
      m. run, turned, washed, shaped   n. walking, speaking, moving, hearing

8. A *Geiger counter* is a o. _____ that measures radioactivity by counting
   the number of charged decay products that p. _____ it.
      o. weapon, device, hammer, ingredient   p. swallow, instigate, strike, trap

9. *Volume* is the amount of q. _____ taken up r. _____ a
   substance.
      q. star, noise, space, knob   r. over, by, under, since

10. A *conductor* is a s. _____ which allows an electric
    t. _____ to flow through it.
       s. material, train, ocean, human   t. train, void, current, shock

Name _____

Weather 'Tis Nobler

Directions: Write down the weather terms defined below. Use the word bank for help. The small boxes, when read from top to bottom, will reveal the atmospheric conditions.

1. streams of light appearing in the northern sky

1. _ _ _ _ _ _ ☐ _ _ _ _ _ _

2. an arc of seven colors created by light refraction through rain droplets

2. _ ☐ _ _ _ _ _

3. a barren area of land receiving very little rainfall

3. _ _ _ ☐ _ _

4. a cloudlike mass lying close to earth

4. _ ☐ _

5. a thick, white fluffy cloud

5. _ _ ☐ _ _ _ _

6. another name for number 8

6. _ _ _ _ _ ☐ _ _

7. a high-speed wind current

7. _ _ _ ☐ _ _ _ _ _

8. a funnel-shaped cloud extension with terrific, whirling, speeding winds

8. _ _ ☐ _ _ _ _

9. a space object often used to form weather predictions

9. _ _ _ _ _ _ ☐ _ _

10. a hot, southerly wind

10. _ _ _ _ ☐ _ _

11. any form of water that falls on the earth's surface

11. _ _ _ _ _ ☐ _ _ _ _ _ _

12. the study of atmosphere and weather

12. _ _ _ _ _ ☐ _ _ _ _ _

13. a frozen form of precipitation

13. _ _ ☐ _ _

14. in Asia, a wind which brings heavy summer rains

14. _ _ _ ☐ _ _ _

15. a brief, sudden violent windstorm

15. ☐ _ _ _ _ _

16. a heavy fall of rain

16. _ _ _ _ _ _ ☐ _

17. liquid precipitation tainted by airborne pollutants

17. _ _ _ _ ☐ _ _ _

18. a warming of the ocean surface off the west coast of South America

18. ☐ _ _ _ _ _

sirocco	satellite	rainbow	jet stream	cumulus	downpour
squall	fog	acid rain	monsoon	cyclone	tornado
Aurora Borealis	precipitation	desert	El Nino	sleet	meteorology

Name _____

Franklin Facts

Directions: Here are paragraphs about the life of patriot Benjamin Franklin. Underline the effect in each cause-and-effect paragraph below. Then choose a title from the box below and write it in the blank to match the paragraph.

1. _____

Josiah Franklin was not a father blinded by his pride. When he saw that his son Ben was unhappy with the family candle-making trade, he sent him to work for an older son.

2. _____

Deborah Read is unable to marry Ben Franklin. This is due to the lack of proof that her long-missing first husband is really dead.

3. _____

Observing Boston's volunteer fire company and noting his own city's problem with fires, Franklin instituted a number of firefighting companies for Philadelphia.

4. _____

Franklin traveled far along the eastern coast of the American colonies to inspect and improve the post offices during his tenure as the colonial Postmaster General.

5. _____

Because Franky, Franklin's second son, died of smallpox at the age of four, Franklin regretted that he had not had the boy inoculated.

6. _____

While experimenting with electrical shock on a turkey, Franklin accidentally shocked himself, knocking himself unconscious for several minutes.

7. _____

Angered by the murder of twenty Indians in 1763, Franklin wrote an attack on the white frontiersman who had killed these helpless victims.

8. _____

Franklin knew that the American colonies, in their quarrels with England, were weak individually. As a result he wrote, "Gentlemen, we must now all hang together, or we shall most assuredly hang separately."

9. _____

Franklin sailed to France because the Americans desperately needed loans for their war with Great Britain.

10. _____

Franklin was puzzled that our young nation, which called for liberty and equality, practiced what he considered the abominable practice of slavery.

Titles

A Loving Father
Uncovering Murder
Improving the Mail
Fighting the Fires Together
A Lost Husband

A Parent Grieves
Finding Financial Aid
An Electric Shock
Banding Together
Liberty for All

---

92   0-7424-0220-7 *Nonfiction Reading Comprehension*

Name _____

Anne Frank's Flight

Directions: Read the selection and answer the questions which follow.

Anne Frank was born into a prosperous German family. She had many friends in her home city of Frankfurt. Her father, Otto, was a businessman. But the Franks were Jews, and when Hitler took power, he started to make anti-Jewish laws. Many German Jews stayed in their homeland, hoping that things would get better, but Otto Frank decided in 1933 that the situation could get dangerous. He opened a branch of his business in Amsterdam and moved his family to Holland.

Anne started to go to school in Amsterdam and made lots of friends. She liked her new school, and she liked acting out stories, writing, and reading. The family spent seven happy years in Holland. But after the outbreak of World War II, Hitler's army conquered and occupied Holland. The same anti-Jewish laws that had caused Otto Frank to flee Germany now had followed them to Amsterdam.

Anne had to leave her school to attend one that had been set up for Jewish students. She and her family had to wear the yellow Star of David on their clothing that identified them as Jews. Day by day, the liberties they had enjoyed were taken from them. But Otto Frank had a plan. He had already started to build a secret annex in the attic of a building he owned for his business. On the day that Anne's older sister, Margot, was told she would have to enter a labor camp, Otto packed up his family and they fled to their new hiding place. Along with her belongings, Anne brought her brand-new diary, which she had just received from her parents as a birthday gift. She was thirteen years old.

For two years, Anne and seven other people—her own family and several family friends—lived in the secret annex. They had to remain still and silent all day long, so that workers in the building below were not able to hear them. Anne found comfort in writing in her diary. She wrote about her cramped life, about the quarrels and difficulties of life in their hiding place, and about her fears and joys.

Anne might have grown up to be a novelist or poet, but that was not to be. On August 4, 1944, the eight hidden Jewish refugees were discovered by German and Dutch Nazi soldiers. They were taken to different concentration camps. Anne Frank died before she reached the age of 16, only a few weeks before the camp was liberated by the British. Otto Frank was the only survivor of the family. He returned to Amsterdam after the war, went back to the secret annex, and found Anne's diary there. In choosing to publish it, Mr. Frank gave us his daughter's beautiful and unique perspective of the war, of the persecution of the Jews, and of the everyday struggles of growing up.

1. Who is the subject of this selection? _____

2. What happened to her and her family? _____

_____

3. Why did Mr. Frank decide to leave Germany? _____

_____

4. Where did the Franks go to escape their enemies?

   a. _____   b. _____

5. Why did they have to go into hiding? _____

6. What was Anne's life like in hiding? _____

_____

7. What did Anne use as comfort during her life in the secret annex?

_____

8. Why is Anne Frank now famous?

_____

9. What would it be like to hide from the world around you for two years?

_____

_____

10. Research: Using different sources, list facts you learn about the Jewish people in World War II.

    Source: _____ _____

    _____

    Source: _____ _____

    _____

    Source: _____ _____

    _____

Name _____

Get into Focus

Directions: Read each group of words. Then order them from general to specific, with the most general being number 1.

1. ___ workers   ___ colony   ___ ant   ___ species

2. ___ book   ___ paragraph   ___ word   ___ chapter

3. ___ reptiles   ___ scale   ___ garter snake   ___ skin covering

4. ___ sun   ___ solar system   ___ galaxy   ___ solar flare

5. ___ coffee plantation   ___ branch   ___ plant   ___ leaf

6. ___ cash register   ___ bank   ___ coin   ___ roll of coins

7. ___ Gobi Desert   ___ sand dune   ___ Asia   ___ grain of sand

8. ___ South Dakota   ___ George Washington   ___ Mt. Rushmore   ___ Washington's nose

9. ___ United States   ___ Washington, D.C.   ___ North America   ___ Pennsylvania Avenue

10. ___ Mr. Adams   ___ Senate   ___ Congress   ___ United States Government

Name _____

Sharpen the Focus

Directions: Read each group of words. Then order them from general to specific, with the most general being number 1.

1. ___ sport   ___ soccer   ___ goalie   ___ defense

2. ___ whisker   ___ tiger   ___ head   ___ cat family

3. ___ mountain   ___ rock   ___ face   ___ range

4. ___ capitol   ___ Australia   ___ Canberra   ___ New South Wales

5. ___ ten   ___ tenth   ___ millionth   ___ hundred

6. ___ Southeast Asia   ___ Java   ___ Jakarta   ___ Indonesia

7. ___ company   ___ worker   ___ division   ___ department

8. ___ room   ___ house   ___ town   ___ neighborhood

9. ___ stalk   ___ swamp life   ___ flower   ___ plant

10. ___ hour   ___ day   ___ second   ___ minute

Name _____

The Battlefield Angel

Directions: Place the bold-print words at the correct points on the time line to note some events of Clara Barton's long and remarkable life.

Clara Barton is well remembered in American history for her work in the terrible War between the States. She cared for wounded, campaigned for nursing supplies, cleaned hospitals, provided food for the patients, traveled through active battlegrounds, and cleaned hospitals. She was a shy, hardworking person. Below are events from her life.

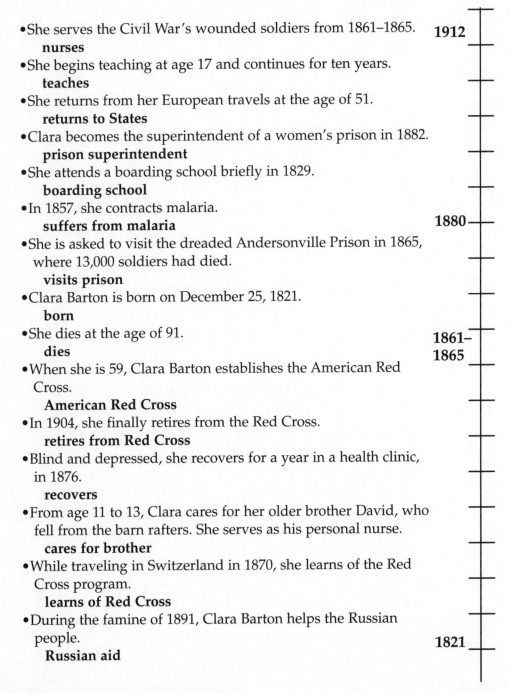

- She serves the Civil War's wounded soldiers from 1861–1865.
  nurses
- She begins teaching at age 17 and continues for ten years.
  teaches
- She returns from her European travels at the age of 51.
  returns to States
- Clara becomes the superintendent of a women's prison in 1882.
  prison superintendent
- She attends a boarding school briefly in 1829.
  boarding school
- In 1857, she contracts malaria.
  suffers from malaria
- She is asked to visit the dreaded Andersonville Prison in 1865, where 13,000 soldiers had died.
  visits prison
- Clara Barton is born on December 25, 1821.
  born
- She dies at the age of 91.
  dies
- When she is 59, Clara Barton establishes the American Red Cross.
  American Red Cross
- In 1904, she finally retires from the Red Cross.
  retires from Red Cross
- Blind and depressed, she recovers for a year in a health clinic, in 1876.
  recovers
- From age 11 to 13, Clara cares for her older brother David, who fell from the barn rafters. She serves as his personal nurse.
  cares for brother
- While traveling in Switzerland in 1870, she learns of the Red Cross program.
  learns of Red Cross
- During the famine of 1891, Clara Barton helps the Russian people.
  Russian aid

1912

1880

1861–
1865

1821

Name _____

Facts About Japan

Directions: Below are facts about the country of Japan. Decide whether each fact describes location L, place P, work/interaction W, or the culture C and place the letter symbol in the blank next to the fact.

1) LOCATION—This explains the address of a land region.
2) PLACE—This includes the location's physical features; it will note the weather, geography, and animals and plants of a region.
3) WORK/INTERACTION—This will explain how people live, govern, and relate to their region.
4) CULTURE—This explains the history, beliefs, and customs of the region's people.

_____ 1. Japan is located off the coasts of Russia, China, and the Koreas.

_____ 2. Women gained equality with men in 1947.

_____ 3. *Shogi* is a board game similar to the game of chess.

_____ 4. Japan has weather similar to that of the east coast of the United States.

_____ 5. Forests cover more than 60 percent of the land.

_____ 6. Japan produces about 11 million vehicles per year.

_____ 7. Kite flying, popular two hundred years ago, still receives much attention.

_____ 8. Japan is a democracy.

_____ 9. Mount Fuji, at 12,388 feet, is the highest point in Japan.

_____ 10. Japan has 250 volcanoes; dozens are active today.

_____ 11. Japanese students attend school five and a half days per week.

_____ 12. Twenty-three percent of all workers are employed by factories.

_____ 13. More than one half of Japan's people practice the religion of Shinto or "the way of the *kami*."

_____ 14. Soccer and baseball are very popular in the country.

_____ 15. The red-crowned crane, or *tancho*, is Japan's national bird.

Name _____

An Ancient Land

Directions: Below are facts about the country of India. Decide whether each fact describes location L, place P, work/interaction W, or the culture C and place the letter symbol in the blank next to the fact.

1) LOCATION—This explains the address of a land region.
2) PLACE—This includes the location's physical features; it will note the weather, geography, and animals and plants of a region.
3) WORK/INTERACTION—This will explain how people live, govern, and relate to their region.
4) CULTURE—This explains the history, beliefs, and customs of the region's people.

_____ 1. Mumbai (formerly Bombay) is well known for the clothing it produces.

_____ 2. Nine hundred million people live in India.

_____ 3. The national animal of India is the tiger. It is protected by law.

_____ 4. One of the world's oldest civilizations, India has 5,000 years of recorded history.

_____ 5. India is a subcontinent peninsula south of the Himalayas.

_____ 6. The most popular sport in India is cricket.

_____ 7. Three quarters of all Indian people are Hindu. Most of them will not eat meat.

_____ 8. The main garment of Indian women is the *sari*.

_____ 9. A major problem in India is overpopulation.

_____ 10. Calcutta, the largest city, has more than 10 million people.

_____ 11. India is the world's largest exporter of tea and spices.

_____ 12. New Delhi is the capital of this democratic country.

_____ 13. The city of Bangalore produces many computers.

_____ 14. The British ruled parts of India from 1686–1947.

_____ 15. The stringed instrument known as the *sitar* comes from India.

Name _____

Bears Compared

Directions: Read the story and answer the questions that follow.

Grizzly and polar bears are large, powerful bears that are similar in many ways, and yet different in others. The habitat of the grizzly bear is western North America. Grizzlies are primarily found in Alaska and western Canada but also can be found in Idaho, Montana, Washington, and Wyoming. Polar bears live mainly along the northern coasts of Alaska, Canada, Greenland, and the Soviet Union. They also inhabit some islands in the Arctic Ocean.

Polar bears hunt seals and other animals such as lemmings, sea birds, and fish for food. But they also eat berries and grasses. Grizzlies feed mainly on land animals, fish, berries, grasses, roots, and leaves.

Grizzlies are brown with thick underfur that can range in color from light tan to almost black. Polar bears have dense, white fur. Beneath their skin is a thick layer of fat that protects them from the fierce cold. Their white fur also serves as camouflage.

Both grizzlies and polar bears live in dens during the cold winter months. In their dens, female polar bears usually give birth to twins. Grizzlies give birth to one or two cubs. The newborn grizzly cubs weigh about one pound (0.5 kilograms) and stay with their mother for one and a half to three and a half years. The newborn polar bear cubs weigh about one and a half pounds (0.68 kilograms) and live with their mother about two years.

Adult male polar bears reach from eight to eleven feet (2.4 to 3.4 meters) long. Some weigh up to 1,000 pounds (454 kilograms). Female polar bears are about six feet (1.8 meters) long and weigh about 400 to 500 pounds (181 to 227 kilograms). Adult grizzlies measure from six to eight feet (1.8 to 2.4 meters) long. Adult males weigh from 400 to 500 pounds (181 to 227 kilograms), while adult female grizzlies weigh in at 350 to 400 pounds (158 to 181 kilograms).

1. List two ways that polar bears and grizzlies are similar and two ways that they differ.

_____

_____

2. How does the size of adult males and adult females of both types of bear differ?

_____

3. On another sheet, create a Venn diagram to compare and contrast polar bears and grizzlies.

4. Research two other types of bears and write a two- to three-paragraph article that compares the two.

Name _____

Norse Traditions

Directions: Read the selection and answer the questions which follow.

(1) Viking families ground their grain into flour using a tool called a *quern*. A quern consisted of two circular stones, one on top of the other. Grain was placed between the two stones and the top stone was turned manually to crush the grain into flour.

(2) Viking men wore flat-heeled leather shoes, which they tied at their ankles with leather strips. They also wore tight-fitting trousers made from sheep wool. Their shirts or tops were long-sleeved tunics which might reach down to their knees. Sometimes this tunic would be worn open at the neck. The Vikings did not have pockets.

(3) Most Vikings were farmers, at least part of the time. Because they lived far from towns, they not only grew their own crops, but they also built their own homes and made their own tools. They grew grains for their bread, harvested fruits such as apples and cherries, planted vegetable crops of onions and peas, raised sheep, cattle, and pigs, and tended geese and chickens.

(4) These people believed that the earth, which they called *Midgard*, was an island in a deep sea full of dangerous monsters. Beneath the earth was a miserably cold land known as *Niflheim*. If a Viking died in bed, he would be transported there in a boat made from the clippings of one's toenails.

(5) Viking long ships were famous for their raised prows and square sails. They might be as much as 100 feet long with a flat, wooden deck. Many of these ships carried tents to provide some protection from the cold and wet. The long ships carried many oars, allowing the sailors to escape their enemies quickly. Unlike most Europeans of their time, these sailors apparently did not fear leaving the sight of land.

Write the paragraph number which relates these terms.

1. ____ pockets
2. ____ Midgard
3. ____ monster

4. ____ oars
5. ____ quern
6. ____ poultry

7. ____ tunic
8. ____ square sail
9. ____ Niflheim

Which paragraph might have each of the following titles?

10. ____ Island Home
11. ____ Fearless Sailors
12. ____ Viking Fashions

13. ____ Grinding Bread
14. ____ Farm Life

15. What was a unique feature of Viking clothing? _____

16. How might ships protect against the cold? _____

17. What name did the Vikings give to the earth? _____

18. What was the shape of a quern stone? _____

19. What occupation did most Vikings have? _____

Name _____

A Pioneer Childhood

Directions: Read the selection and then answer the questions.

Most people would include Abraham Lincoln's name in the list of the greatest United States Presidents. His leadership during the Civil War and his vision of "a more perfect union" in a time of trouble are even more impressive because Lincoln had little formal education and came from a humble background. What do we know about Lincoln's early life?

Lincoln attended a school in Indiana for, by his own estimate, only a total of a few years. But he loved to learn and read every book he could find in his wilderness neighborhood. One time, Lincoln's teacher told him that he should learn grammar. Lincoln walked twelve miles to get a copy of a grammar book, which he then learned by heart. He also memorized most of *Robinson Crusoe*.

Lincoln's love of word started to show early in his life; he loved jokes and stories. When he went to country dances, he was often the center of attention while he told funny stories and tales from the books he had read. This friendly and witty nature served him well. In fact, during one political debate with a senator, Lincoln was called "two-faced." Lincoln smiled and said, "I leave it to my audience. If I had another face, do you think I'd be wearing this one?"

The Lincoln family was a pioneer family with few possessions, but they did not lack for essentials—food, warmth, and shelter. They lived in a country that offered free land, free timber to build homes, free wood to heat those homes, and all of the food they could hunt and raise. After Abraham Lincoln's mother died, his father married again. The second Mrs. Lincoln brought pots, pans, and furniture to their rustic cabin. She brought something else, too: a respect for books and schooling, which she passed on to her stepchildren. Years afterward, Lincoln fondly recalled the important part she played in his remarkable life.

1. Write a list of four personality traits or abilities that Lincoln showed during his childhood:

_____   _____

_____   _____

2. Why do you think Lincoln had to walk so far to borrow books to read?

_____

3. What was the most important thing that Lincoln's stepmother brought with her when she married into the Lincoln family?

_____

4. Circle the word from the story that means *untrustworthy* or *deceitful*:

humble   **essential**   **two-faced**   **rustic**

Name _____

State Your Case

Directions: Fill out the puzzle below; the circled letters are the answer to the question.

In 1986 the three-cornered hat on the William Penn statue in Philadelphia was no longer the highest point in the city. What was?

1. W _ _ _ _ N _
2. _ _ C H _ _ _ _
3. N _ _ _ Y _ _ _ _
4. _ _ _ _ N _ _ S
5. _ _ _ Z _ _ A
6. _ _ _ B _ M _
7. M _ _ _ _ _
8. _ _ S S _ _ R _
9. _ _ _ H
10. _ _ _ _ _ _ C _ Y
11. _ _ _ _ H _ _ _ _ H _ _ _ _
12. _ _ _ _ F _ _ N _ _ _
13. _ E _ _ _ _
14. _ L _ _ A _ _ _
15. _ W _ _ R _ _ _ _

Answer: _____

Clues:
1. state of the Grand Tetons
2. state of the Mackinac Bridge
3. state of the Erie Canal
4. state of the Windy City
5. state of Meteor Crater
6. state with the capital Birmingham
7. state of Acadia National Park
8. state of the Gateway Arch
9. state of Rainbow Bridge, a natural stone bridge
10. state of Mammoth Cave
11. state of the Old Man of the Mountain
12. state of Mount Whitney
13. state that honors Sam Houston
14. state of Mesa Verde National Park
15. state connected to NYC by the Lincoln Tunnel

Extra: There are 35 states not mentioned in this puzzle. Can you think of five additional state facts? For this exercise and the one above, use other resources if you need help.

Name _____

Woolly Mammoth

Directions: In the report below, every sentence has one or two words that are added or changed to make the information false. Use common sense and, if you wish, additional resource material, to correct the report. Write your corrections editorial-style, in the spaces between the lines.

Report on the Woolly Mammoth

The woolly mammoth had a very thin coat of shaggy hair. It needed this coat to live in the northern parts of Asia, Hawaii, Europe, North America, and South America. It lived long ago during the Industrial Age. The early mammal was the first form of elephant to have lived on the earth. The woolly mammoth was about ten feet wide and weighed up to eight pounds.

Even though the last of this species probably died out 10,000 months ago, we know much about the beast. Because some mammoths have been preserved in glacial ice for thousands of years, we have no fine specimen to examine.

The mammoth was a carnivore and ate a diet of leaves from trees and bushes. We think that one of the uses of their long tails was to clear snow from the ground to reach their food sources. The animal's three-inch layer of fat gave it added insulation in a hot climate. The fat also served as a food supply during the bleak summer months when little food could be found.

Name _____

Knightly Words

Directions: Match the terms from the word bank to their correct definitions.

The medieval days of knights, castles, and feats of bravery are fascinating and have inspired many stories and songs. Some of the most familiar words from this era of history are defined below. Use a dictionary if you need help matching words to definitions.

_____ 1. a steel-tipped spear used by knights on horseback

_____ 2. interlinked, ringed armor

_____ 3. horseback combat using lances

_____ 4. horse-riding warrior troops

_____ 5. the home and land owned by a lord

_____ 6. the family design on armor or a banner

_____ 7. the shield-bearer and helper of a knight

_____ 8. the front piece of a helmet

_____ 9. water encircling a castle to protect it

_____ 10. a ceremony in which a squire is knighted

_____ 11. the traditions and spirit of knighthood

_____ 12. the servant who trains the knight's hawks for hunting

Word Bank		
cavalry	dubbing	squire
chain mail	lance	moat
manor	chivalry	joust
visor	crest	falconer

Name _____

What's the Point?

Directions: Can you match the moral to each story? Here are summaries of five of Aesop's fables. Choose the moral from the list on page 107 that best fits each story.

Aesop, the author of many famous fables, or teaching stories, is a figure of mystery. We know almost nothing about the writer who created the characters and scenes which we still read and discuss today. The famous historian Herodotus said that Aesop had lived in the sixth century B.C., a slave to a wealthy man. Another author, Plutarch, insisted that Aesop had lived in the first century A.D., and was an advisor to King Croesus of Lydia, the wealthiest man of that era. In one way, it doesn't matter that we know so little about the historical Aesop, because we have the treasure of his fables. Each one comes with a *moral*, a lesson that we can learn from the story. Read descriptions of some of Aesop's work below and decide which moral goes with each tale.

1. In the fable, "The Mountain in Labor," a mountain began to rumble. All the people had suggestions as to why the mountain shook and roared. Some said that the gods were angry. Others claimed that the mountain was in labor and about to give birth. Still others feared that the world was coming to an end. Each theory grew increasingly nonsensical as the mountain's roar increased and the earth shook. Finally, the noisy mountain burst open, and there appeared—a mouse.

   Moral: _____

2. In the tale "Venus and the Cat," it was the time of the gods. A beautiful young cat fell in love with a young man. When her love grew unbearable, the cat approached the goddess of love and asked if she might be turned into a human. Venus agreed. The cat girl was beautiful and caught the young man with her many charms. They were wed. Over time Venus became curious. How was the couple doing? So she came down to spy on them. Ah, she thought to herself, has the girl truly changed her habits? Venus released a mouse, which scampered in sight of the girl. Seeing the mouse, the girl pounced upon it, ready to eat the rodent. Venus then changed the girl back into a cat.

   Moral: _____

   _____

3. A widow has two irresponsible and lazy servant girls in "The Old Woman and Her Maids." Because of the widow's diligent guidance, the maids did hard work, but they hated it! Every day they rose with the crowing rooster. And so they devised a plan. Hoping to lengthen their hours of sleep, the two girls secretly kill the rooster. But since the widow could no longer depend on a rooster's crowing to start her day, she woke her servants even earlier. The two maids then had to work long before the rising of the sun.

Moral: _____

_____

4. In "The Piping Fisherman" we read about a musically gifted young man who prefers music to money. He hoped to make the creatures of the sea dance to the playing of his pipes. But none would dance or frolic to his magnificent music. And so he went to work and cast his fishing net into the sea. After pulling the net to shore, the fisherman spied a vast quantity of fishes who seem to dance and leap into the open air. "Ah," said the young man sadly, "you dance too late so you shall dance no more."

Moral: _____

List of Morals:
Magnificent promises are not always matched by performance.
Too much cunning can have unfortunate results.
It is a great art to do the right thing at the right time.
One can change one's appearance but not one's nature.

Name _____

Silent Sentinels

Directions: Read the story and answer the questions which follow.

Some lands are associated with their animals. Mention kangaroos and the country of Australia comes to mind. Some lands may be tied to their foods. Hear the word *pasta* and one thinks of Italy. But few lands are brought to mind through their stones. One is Easter Island, the land of the giant *moai*.

In the South Pacific, on the furthest eastern reaches of the Polynesian group which includes Hawaii, Tahiti, and New Zealand, is Easter Island. This forlorn and often forgotten island was formed by the eruptions of three volcanoes at least a million years ago. Its nearest neighbors are Pitcairn Island 1,400 miles to the west and the Chilean coast 2,200 miles eastward. Chile governs the island today. Forests once covered the island, but even before the first Europeans came, Easter Island's wooded plains disappeared, leaving a bare, treeless land which is as we see it today.

"Easter Island" is the name given the isle since the arrival of the Dutch sea captain Jacob Roggeveen, who landed on April 5, 1722—Easter Sunday. The island's Polynesian name, *Rapa Nui*, is also the name of its natives and past language.

The Polynesians, the first settlers of this land, sailed from the western islands in long canoes around A.D. 400. They were remarkable sailors, well trained to study the stars, who understood bird flight patterns, the winds, and the water currents. The clans which settled upon the island were ruled by their priests, or *ariki*. As each family group competed with its neighbors for position and power, alliances were formed to ensure their goals and privileges. Each kinship group included priests, warriors, craftsmen, farmers, and fishermen.

A unique custom of the Rapanui, which developed over time, was a festival which coincided with the yearly arrival of a particular bird, the tern. The birds and their eggs were obviously sources of food; the islanders eagerly awaited their coming. With the birds' arrival each clan chose a healthy, athletic young man to represent them in competition. Each selected contestant would swim out to one of three nesting islands, grab an egg, and return with it undamaged. He would offer this egg to his clan leader. The clan leader who received an egg first was declared the *tangata manu*, or birdman, for the following year. He was seen as the human representative of Makemake, the creator god, and he would rule the island for the next 12 moons.

But what about the *moai*? The *moai* were large statues carved from the volcanic Rano Raraku. The islander clans showed reverence to their *moai*, which they believed possessed powers but were not gods. It is thought that these statues represented ancestors from the various clans. The images varied in shape and size, but the average *moai* was roughly 20 feet high and might weigh several tons. Set with large noses, elongated ears, thin lips, large foreheads, and cylindrical torsos, the *moai* loomed over the grassy landscape upon their altar plains, or *ahu*.

The skilled sculptors who crafted the *moai* were highly praised by their communities. Stone work was their only work. Others provided their food and housing needs. The images were carved out at the Rano Raraku quarry, polished with coral, somehow moved miles away, raised, and tipped into place upon the raised platform of the clan's *ahu*. Some *moai*, it is believed, were then painted. Most *moai* face inland, their backs to the sea.

What happened to these islanders? And why were all *moai* tipped on their faces when the Europeans arrived? According to tradition, the various clans had fierce wars and conflicts as their food sources and natural resources dwindled in supply. Supposedly, victorious clans cannibalized their victims. Opposing clans would deface and overthrow the *moai* of their enemies until none were left standing.

We do know that in 1862 more than 1,000 Rapanui were captured as slaves to be sold in Peru as miners. After the church intervened and won their freedom, the 100-plus survivors were shipped back to Easter Island where they infected their families with smallpox. Only a few hundred islanders survived the plague. Most moved to Tahiti in the 1870s.

Today many of the *moai* have been raised again, silent sentinels on an island the world has all but forgotten.

1. How was the island formed? _____

2. Who were the first settlers? _____

3. When did they arrive? _____

4. Where is Easter Island? _____

5. Describe the birdman ceremony. _____

   _____

6. What name is given to the large stone statues? _____

7. What do you suppose would be the hardest work in preparing the statues? Why? _____

   _____

8. What awful thing happened in 1862? _____

9. What is the Polynesian name for this island? _____

Name _____

Cave Life

Directions: As you read the statements below, circle the one word in parentheses which best completes each factual statement. Use an encyclopedia if you need help.

1. Scientists who study caves and work to (**leak   pretend   discover**) how they were formed are called *speleologists*.

2. Sometimes, as a volcano (**dies   erupts   lightens**), it pours out liquid rock called *lava*. As it flows away, the lava's surface may (**cool   burn   shine**) much faster than the lava on the inside. Then the outer lava hardens and the inner lava flows off (**leaving   signing   carrying**) an empty middle. A *lava-tube cave* is formed.

3. At other times waves crashing into the stony cliffs of the shore (**save   step   scoop**) out or wear away the softer (**water   rock   sand**) and form *sea caves*.

4. Limestone and sandstone caves are made from the remains of ancient ocean floors. Over (**mountains   space   time**), forces below the surface of the (**earth   mesa   equator**) push these old ocean floors up above the sea. Rivers create passageways and canyons (**beyond   through   against**) the rock.

5. Although green plants (**summon   demand   encourage**) sunlight, fungi can (**show   send   obtain**) their energy from nutrient-rich water, animal droppings, or dead plants and animals. For example, a mushroom may (**sprout   die   bake**) from the droppings or *guano* of bats.

6. Quite a few (**genders   traits   species**) of animals live in caves. These creatures, which include the cave crab, are called *troglobites* and do not necessarily need to (**see   grow   walk**) well. Some may have no eyes at all. Most troglobites have excellent touch and smell (**equipment   sensors   feet**).

7. Other animals, living in caves (**only   when   after**) part time, are called *trogloxenes*. This means that they are cave guests. Such creatures, such as the (**frog   squirrel   bat**), the bear, and the bobcat, may sleep or raise their (**flag   young   hand**) in the caves but search for food above ground.

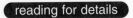

Name _____

Must Be Santa

Directions: Read the story and answer the questions which follow.

There was a real Saint Nicholas. He grew up in the Turkish town of Lycia in the early fourth century A.D. After his parents died, he joined the church and eventually became a bishop. A story is told about a boat trip during which Nicholas was caught in a terrible storm. The legend says that Nicholas raised his arms and the sea was stilled.

Bishop Nicholas was put into prison during the persecution of Christians in Roman Europe, but he was freed by the new emperor, Constantine. Two of the bishop's reported qualities are still known to us today. First, he was said to be an very generous person. Second, he showed deep love for the children in his world. In some stories of the saint, he would throw bags of coins down the chimneys of families in need.

Over the next thousand years, Nicholas was given a saint's day, December 6. More legends were added to the historical accounts of his life. But during the Reformation of the 1500s, his legend nearly disappeared.

But Dutch children still placed their wooden shoes by the family hearth on the evening of December 5. These shoes were filled with straw to feed the saint's donkey. Children believed that Nicholas would replace the straw with a small treat. The Dutch spelled the saint's name *Sint Nikolass*. When the Dutch came to the Americas, they brought these traditions to New Amsterdam. The English, who wrestled the land from them, changed the region's name to New York and the saint's name to Santa Claus.

Santa's reindeer joined the ongoing legend when a family friend took a doctor's poem, written for his children, and sent it to a newspaper. Dr. Moore's *The Night Before Christmas* changed everyone's image about the ancient saint. For more than 1,500 years, Saint Nicholas was viewed as a tall, noble figure in long robes. An American cartoonist of the mid-nineteenth century named Thomas Nash drew images of Santa for the *Harper's Weekly* magazine, based on Moore's poem. Nash altered our image of Nicholas forever. Santa is now a round and bearded person in a red suit and boots, but he is still a giver of gifts with a great love of children.

1. Saint Nicholas was born in the city of _____.

2. He became a _____ after the death of his parents.

3. Saint Nicholas was in prison until he was freed by _____.

4. This saint's special day is _____.

5. Dutch children placed _____ by the hearth to welcome the saint.

6. *Santa Claus* comes from the Dutch name _____.

7. Dr. Moore wrote the poem _____ in 1822.

8. The image we have of Santa is from the work of Thomas Nash, a _____.

9. Question: Why do you think Santa Claus is so popular to children and adults today?

_____

Name _____

Idioms

Directions: Write the idiom from the bank to describe the mood of each quote.

Idioms are expressions that develop in specific countries or regions, and which enrich language with unusual turns of phrase. Idioms usually express a feeling vividly.

1. "I'm so sorry. I was wrong to believe that."

    _____

2. "We got very little money for our antique brass lamp."

    _____

3. "He made no sense when he shared his story."

    _____

4. "So, you wish to be a professional ball player. So do many other people!"

    _____

5. "You're getting all upset about your homework."

    _____

6. "I hope she calls soon. I'm having a hard time waiting."

    _____

7. "When Sean couldn't get his way, he quit."

    _____

8. "I'm going to sleep for a short time."

    _____

9. "May I have the extra pie?"

    _____

10. "I really can't help you at all."

    _____

Idiom Bank

bark up the wrong tree	catch 40 winks
dime a dozen	on pins and needles
eat humble pie	get into a stew
sell for a song	licking one's chops
throw in the towel	talk in circles

Name _____

Punxsutawney Phil

Directions: Read the story and answer the questions which follow.

Does the groundhog really know when spring will come? Where does this superstition come from? And what is all this tradition about February 2?

Let's start with spring's arrival. The groundhog has no inkling of the coming of spring. After a period of hibernation, the mammal is well rested and has its appetite to consider. Groundhogs put on weight before hibernation and the body feeds off this extra weight all winter. If it is sufficiently awake, the now-thin animal will wander out looking for some food. If, however, the groundhog is only partially awake, it will most likely roll over and go back to sleep.

The Germans had an old tradition about the animal and its shadow. Of course, their beast was a bit larger and more European—it was the badger. So why did we get the groundhog for the story? In the nineteenth century, a group of German immigrants settled in and around the town of Punxsutawney, Pennsylvania. They knew their folklore; they enjoyed their traditions. But Punxsutawney had no badgers, so they looked for the closest native animal they could find: the groundhog. A new tradition was born.

Now for the date. Groundhogs living in warmer climates generally awaken in January. Groundhogs whose habitats lie to the north and Upper Great Lakes areas may not budge from their nests until March. Punxsutawney groundhogs just happen to awaken around February 2.

So, is the groundhog a trustworthy predictor of spring's arrival? No. Its 28 percent accuracy rate leaves lots of room for improvement.

1. Why does the groundhog leave its nest? _____
2. Why is the groundhog our chosen spring predictor? _____
3. What animal originally was used in this tradition? _____
4. Who came to Punxsutawney in the nineteenth century? _____
5. What word in the selection is another word for *accurate*? _____
6. Do all groundhogs awaken on February 2? _____
7. How often is the groundhog's prediction wrong?_____
8. What do you think would be a better predictor of springtime?_____
    Why? _____

Name _____

Historically Thinking

Directions: Each of the quotes below has three or four blanks. Fill in the blanks with the words found in parentheses.

---

1. Executive Oath of Office: "I do _____ swear (or affirm) that I will faithfully _____ the Office of President of the United States, and will to the best of my ability, _____, protect and defend the Constitution of the United States."
   —United States Constitution, Article II, Section 1, Clause 8

   (execute, preserve, solemnly)

2. My _____ citizens of the world: ask not what _____ will do for you, but what together we can do for the _____ of man.
   —John F. Kennedy, Inaugural Address, January 20, 1961

   (America, fellow, freedom)

3. Four _____ and seven years ago, our fathers brought forth upon this continent a new nation: _____ in liberty, and dedicated to the _____ that all men are created equal.
   —Abraham Lincoln, Gettysburg Address, given November 19, 1863

   (proposition, score, conceived)

4. I am _____ aware that you have not elected me as your President by your _____, and so I ask you to confirm me as your _____ with your prayers.
   —Gerald R. Ford, remarks after taking the oath of office of the President, August 9, 1974

   (acutely, President, and ballots)

5. Let us therefore _____ ourselves to our _____, and so bear ourselves that if the British Empire and its Commonwealth last for a thousand years, men will still say, 'This was their _____ hour.'
   —Winston Churchill, speech made on June 18, 1940

   (finest, brace, duties)

6. "We, the people of the United States, in order to form a more perfect union, establish justice, _____ domestic tranquillity, provide for the common defense, promote the general _____, and secure the blessings of liberty to ourselves and our posterity, do _____ and establish this Constitution for the United States of America."

      —Preamble to the United States Constitution

(insure, welfare, ordain)

7. I know not what _____ others may take; but as for me, give me _____, or give me _____!

      —Patrick Henry, speech made on March 23, 1775

(death, liberty, course)

8. Hear me, my _____! I am tired; my heart is _____ and sad. From where the sun now stands I will fight no more _____.

      —Chief Joseph, address made in 1877

(sick, forever, Chiefs)

Name _____

Lucky Charms

Directions: Read the story and answer the questions which follow.

We humans are superstitious. It is the result of our desire for security in an insecure world. Many cultures and traditions play a part in our superstitions. For example, what's so lucky about a horseshoe?

According to one fable from Europe, there lived a blacksmith named Dunstan. A visitor came to him one day, asking to have horseshoes attached to his feet. Puzzled, Dunstan asked to see that man's feet. The guest pulled up his trousers to reveal two cloven hooves. Dunstan realized instantly that his visitor was the Devil. Dunstan then tricked the devil into agreeing to be chained to the wall for the shoeing. Once Dunstan had the upper hand, he made the Devil promise never to enter any house that had a horseshoe nailed to its wall. For many years people in the British Isles celebrated St. Dunstan's Day, May 19, with a game of horseshoes.

How about knocking on wood? Today we knock on wood to mean "let it be so!" But this tradition is very old. Among the Native Americans—even before the Greeks started the habit—trees were homes to the spirits, and the oak tree was especially sacred. These people noted that lightning often struck the oak, and they thought that the oak was the home to their sky god. These tribes believed that bragging about their future—victories, accomplishments, or bounty—would result in failure. If a person caught himself talking too hopefully, he would rap upon the trunk of the oak tree to tell the spirit of the tree that he was sorry for speaking so rashly.

1. What does *cloven* mean? _____

2. Give a synonym for the word *trousers*. _____

3. Why do people hang horseshoes? _____

4. What does it mean today when we knock on wood? _____
   _____

5. Why did Native Americans think that the oak was the home of the sky god? _____
   _____
   _____

Name _____

A Crown of Wild Olive Leaves

Directions: Read the selections and fill in each blank with the correct homophones.

Imagine yourself as spectator at the ancient Greek games! Use the word bank of homophones to fill in each blank within the sentence. Then use the other homophone in the pair to write your own sentence on the line provided. Try to write sentences about the Olympics.

Word Bank			
all—awl	scent—sent	waits—weights	site—sight
throne—thrown	way—weigh	him—hymn	toes—tows
mail—male	scene—seen	war—wore	one—won

1. In the ancient games all athletes were _____. Unmarried women were allowed to attend the spectacle, but married women were not.

   _____

2. The _____ for the games was chosen carefully so that it was in full view of an important landmark.

   _____

3. The temple of Zeus could be _____ from the Games. The games were dedicated in honor of this god.

   _____

4. One _____ that athletes relaxed was to swim in the pool at Olympia. But there were no swimming races in this one-and-only pool of ancient Greece.

   _____

5. Every four years, three heralds would be _____ from the town of nearby Elis to proclaim the games and announce the *Olympic Truce*.

   _____

6. These heralds carried staffs and _____ wreaths of olive leaves.

   _____

7. The long-jump participants carried heavy lead _____. Yet distances of over 16 meters were recorded!

   _____

   _____

8. The greatest honor was given to the winner of the stade. This was a run equal to about 192 meters. The winning sprinter had that year's Games named after _____.

_____

9. Runners began from a standing start, feet together, _____ gripping the grooves in the stone slabs which served as the starting line.

_____

10. Wrestlers _____ their events if their opponent had three falls. A fall was declared any time a wrestler's back or shoulder touched the ground.

_____

11. The Olympic Games were one of four all-Greek sports competitions. These games were open to _____ Greek men. At the all-Athens games, one event familiar to us today was a torch race.

_____

12. One chariot competitor, Emperor Nero, won his event even though he was _____ from his vehicle and failed to finish. Bribing the judges, Nero was named the champion with the excuse that he would have won if he had finished! After he died, the judges returned the bribe money.

_____

Name _____

Food! Glorious Food!

Directions: Ever wonder where our food ideas came from? Here is some trivia for you. Circle the letter of the correct conclusion at the end of each paragraph.

1. The pancake comes to us from Ancient Egypt, perhaps about 2600 B.C. When they learned to leaven their gruel with yeast, the Egyptians invented ovens for their bread. Their pancakes were made of the same ingredients, minus the leaven, but cooked the old-fashioned way—on top of the stove.

   From this paragraph we know that . . .
   a. Pancakes are hard.   c. Americans created pancakes.
   b. Egyptians loved gruel.   d. Ovens were invented in Egypt.

2. The sausage had its birth in Babylonia. The eating of sausage was actually outlawed in much of Europe for centuries, but it later returned as a food of choice. In Vienna, butchers made *vieners* or *wieners*. The butcher guilds of Frankfurt came up with the variation called *frankfurters*. The *dachshund sausage* made its way to America and was renamed here again. It was a cartoonist, Tad Dorgan, who sketched a dachshund dog smeared with mustard and wrapped in a bun as a joke one day as he watched a baseball game. The name "hot dog" was the result of this popular cartoon. We've enjoyed our hot dogs ever since, especially at baseball games.

   The sausage was . . .
   a. made from dogs.   c. always unlawful.
   b. called by many names.   d. created by Tad Dorgan.

3. One hundred fifty years ago, George Crum worked as a chef at a summer resort in Saratoga Springs, New York. At the time, French-fried potatoes were extremely popular. Everyone seemed to ask for them at the fancy restaurants of the resort town. One day, a customer complained that the fries Crum cooked were too thick and requested a second platter. But these, too, were rejected by the guest. Crum, frustrated by the two-time failure of a simple order, decided to give this customer something different. He cut the fries very thin. He crisped them so thoroughly that they could not be eaten with a fork. But the formerly fuming customer loved the chips of potato. Crum had started a new house specialty, the potato chip.

   George Crum was not . . .
   a. a creator.   c. a frustrated worker.
   b. a chef.   d. a dishwasher.

4. You must go to the China of 2000 B.C. to find the earliest ice cream. The Chinese nobility loved this specialty milk creation. Its ingredients were overcooked rice, spices, and milk, which were mixed and hardened in snow. Over the centuries ice-cream recipes changed, but ice-cream manufacture remained a slow, painstaking process until the 1560s, when a doctor in Rome found a way to freeze the cream mixture quickly by adding saltpeter to snow or ice. The new ease of making ice cream caused it to be served more often. By the time Thomas Jefferson returned to the United States after serving as ambassador to France, it was a favorite gourmet dessert. Jefferson brought home a prized ice-cream-making machine.

No mention is made here of ice cream in . . .

    a. China.   **c. Antarctica.**

    b. the United States.   **d. Rome.**

5. The Greeks had the idea of baking pies, but we would not recognize them as such. Their pies did not have a top crust, and were filled with meat or fish. The Romans added the top layer of crust. They also liked to put honey, spices, and sheep-milk cheeses in the filling. It was not until the reign of Queen Elizabeth I of England that fruit fillings were used. It is said that Queen Elizabeth loved her cherry pies!

This paragraph mentions . . .

    a. five filling ingredients.   **c. seven filling ingredients.**

    b. six filling ingredients.   **d. eight filling ingredients.**

6. Do you like to eat popcorn at the movie theater? It is an original North American treat. In fact, Columbus received popcorn necklaces on his voyages to the New World. Popcorn was brought to the first Thanksgiving meal in 1621 in deerskin bags. Some Native Americans had an interesting way of enjoying this food. They would poke a stick through an ear of popcorn and heat the ear over a fire. As the kernels popped and flew up in the air, people caught the popcorn to eat!

From this paragraph you can tell that . . .

    a. Columbus loved popcorn.

    b. Popcorn needed to be salted.

    c. Popcorn was first made by Native Americans.

    d. Thanksgiving began with popcorn.

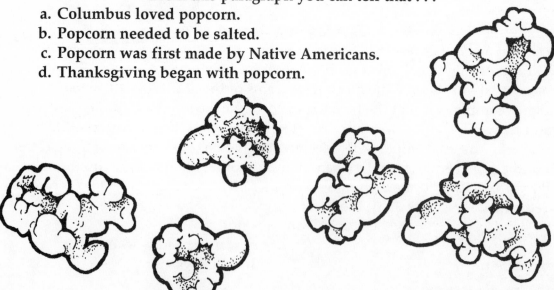

Answer Key

A Day in a Different World   page 6
1. soccer
2. groundskeeper, sell cloth, guard property
3. Answers will vary.
4. tortillas, rice, beans, chicken, vegetables, coffee, corn bread, fruit
5. Answers will vary but may include one room, heated with wood stove, use sleeping mats for bedding
6. Answers will vary.

Home Sweet Home   page 8
1.   a. T, W, B   e. W   i. T   m. W
    b. B   f. B   j. T   n. T
    c. T   g. B   k. B   o. W
    d. T   h. T   l. W   p. W
2. protection from predators
3. Answers will vary.
4. Answers will vary by type.
5. Answers will vary.
6. Answers will vary.

My Little Runaway   page 9
1. America, disguises
2. immature, predator
3. leaps, escapes
4. feet, earth
5. feared, clear
6. similar, harmless
7. about, tight
8. writhes, attention
9. spreads, revealing
10. attack, chunk

Common Ground   page 10
1. yard tools
2. names for a dog
3. capital cities
4. rhyming long o words
5. field sports
6. animal sounds
7. states of matter
8. girls' names
9. measuring tools
10. primary colors
11. garden flowers
12. things that jump
13. amphibians
14. mountain ranges
15. board games
16. tropical fruits
17. weather conditions
18. stringed instruments
19. S. American rivers
20. yes

Fascinating Facts   pages 11–12
1. shocked
2. deposits
3. experience
4. equator
5. observe
6. sphere
7. rainfall
8. hot
9. natural gas
10. the Sun
11. level
12. Middle East
13. measured
14. roughly
15. thermometer
16. years

Shall We Dance?   page 14
1. Cuming County, NE/Nemaha, IA
2. tractor drivers dance their machines
3. Answers will vary.
4. prepare 100th anniversary celebration of their town
5. hard times . . . have fun
6. tractors
7. wares—c. goods
    promenade—d. stroll
    bravado—b. reckless bravery
    gingham—a. cotton cloth
8. Answers will vary.

Birds of a Feather   page 15
1. stork
2. weaverbird
3. bowerbird
4. ovenbird
5. ruby-throated hummingbird
6. piping plover
7. peregrine falcon
8. northern oriole

Thirst Quenchers   page 16
1. apple cider
2. lemonade
3. hot chocolate
4. mineral water
5. cranberry juice
6. ice tea
7. orange juice
8. punch
9. grape soda
10. root beer
11. coffee

Earth Shakers   page 17
1. force
2. rock
3. flowing
4. different
5. explode
6. ash
7. ascend
8. glows
9. light
10. eruption
11. captured
12. rapidly
13. five
14. nearby
15. sole

Geography Gems   pages 18
1. plain
2. escarpment
3. lake
4. island
5. plateau
6. tributary
7. peninsula
8. bay
9. isthmus

page 19
1. cataract
2. pass
3. delta
4. strait
5. fauna
6. flora
7. mountain
8. mouth
9. canyon

Starting with D   page 20
1. damsel
2. douse
3. dance
4. diamond
5. dye
6. don
7. drake
8. dirt
9. dog
10. damp
11. date
12. dromedary
13. doleful
14. daisy
15. danger
16. dual
17. damask
18. doubtful
19. dash
20. drought
21. dozen

Victorious   **page 21**
What Diseases—scarlet fever, polio
Years of Life—1940 to 1994
Saddest News—never walk again, school will not accept her
Who—Wilma Rudolph
Where Born—Clarksville, TN
Victories Accomplished—learns to walk, Olympic gold medals
What Sports—track and field, basketball

Scribbling Master   **page 23**
1. Answers will vary.
2. watchtower
3. visited zoos
4. wrote documentary scripts, drew cartoons
5. Answers will vary.
6. *The Cat in the Hat*
   Horton Hears a Who
   mother's maiden name
   The Lorax

My Children Are Hungry   **page 24**
1. F   6. F
2. F   7. T
3. T   8. F
4. F   9. T
5. F   10. T

The Inca   **page 26**
1. An Indian people of South America who ruled one of the largest and richest empires in the Americas.
2. Argentina, Bolivia, Colombia, Chile, Ecuador, and Peru
3. cotton, corn, potatoes, quinoa, oca
4. Answers will vary.
5. Answers will vary.
6. oca—an edible root
   Quechua—the spoken language of the Inca
   amauta—a teacher
   quipu—a cord used to keep records
   panpipe—a musical instrument

A Young Maiden   **page 27**
1. a. 17
   b. 1
   c. 17
   d. 12
   e. 19
2. England
3. Joan is captured and killed.
4. the archangel
5. Vancouleurs
6. Answers will vary.

The Shona   **page 29**
1. l   8. e
2. j   9. g
3. d   10. m
4. i   11. n
5. f   12. k
6. b   13. a
7. h   14. c

Possible Answers:
1. created an empire
2. built stone-walled fortresses
3. traded gold

4. crafted pottery and gold artifacts
5. traded with India and China

Look Closely   **page 30**
1. sunlight—V   7. steam engine—T
2. downstream—S   8. red—E
3. Alpha Centari—B   9. squid—O
4. kangaroo—O   10. Laura I. Wilder—R
5. structure—I   11. larynx—A
6. powder horn—N
   OBSERVATION

Pick Three   **page 31**
1. longitude, equator, latitude; imaginary lines which we use to locate position
2. sleet, rain, hail; forms of precipitation
3. South America, Asia, Europe; continents
4. Oahu, Sri Lanka, Sicily; islands
5. Sudan, Tanzania, Angola; African nations
6. Danube, Orinoco, Euphrates, rivers
7. Atlas, Ural, Sierra Madre; mountain ranges
8. tree, iron, river; natural resources

Which "-ist" Is It?   **page 32**
1. bacteriologist   7. psychologist
2. meteorologist   8. arborist
3. anthropologist   9. optimist
4. biologist   10. optometrist
5. chemist   11. geologist
6. physicist   12. cellist

A Blast from the Past   **page 34**
The events are in order as follows: 7, 5, 4, 1, 3, 6, 2
1. F—change *comet* to *meteorite*
2. T
3. F—change *hit* to *burst above*
4. F—change *afternoon* to *morning*
5. T

Canada   **page 35**
The events are in order as follows:
Northwest Territories—4, 2, 6, 1, 5, 3
Yukon—2, 7, 4, 6, 3, 1, 5
Newfoundland and Labrador—3, 1, 6, 4, 5, 2, 7

Cruising Along   **page 36**
1. steam, wealthy
2. workers, one
3. popular, Volkswagen
4. cool
5. tires, rubber, headlights, replace

In an Orderly Fashion   **page 37**
1. D   7. B   13. B
2. C   8. A   14. A
3. C   9. D   15. B
4. D   10. C   16. D
5. B   11. D
6. C   12. A

How Revolutionary!   **pages 38-39**
1. T, F, *T, F
2. F, *T, T, F
3. *T, T, F, T
4. T, F, *T, F

Women Rule! pages 40-41

Laura Ingalls Wilder—pioneer
James Barry—doctor
Salote Mafile'o Pilolevu—ruler
Wang Yani—painter
Phillis Wheatley—poet

1.	Phillis	8.	Miranda
2.	Yani	9.	Laura
3.	Laura	10.	Phillis
4.	Salote	11.	Salote
5.	Miranda	12.	Phillis
6.	Laura	13.	Yani
7.	Salote	14.	Laura

Do You Believe? page 42–43

1. fetch
2. in a mirror
3. a British clergyman
4. a young boy
5. sickness would come to England
6. Sgt. Griffith's double
7. 1944—saved from machine-gun fire
   1964—saved from fallen tree
8. a line of soldiers

Fact or Fiction page 44

1.	lives	14.	while
2.	Nepal	15.	rescued
3.	modern	16.	nine
4.	might	17.	tall
5.	hired	18.	fed
6.	returned	19.	health
7.	camp	20.	him
8.	mythological	21.	certainly
9.	Foot	22.	furred
10.	unusual	23.	antelope
11.	prints	24.	exists
12.	wide	25.	proof
13.	account		

Space Missiles page 45

1. meteoroids—comets-asteroids
2. comets—asteroids-meteoroids
3. foretelling terrible events
4. a. friction with atmosphere
   b. sunlight on coma
5. very bright meteor
6. meteoroid—a rock or metal space sphere smaller
   than a comet
   meteor—enter Earth's atmosphere
   meteorite—a meteoroid that lands on Earth

The Adventurers page 47

1. Dogs and humans trek across Arctic Ocean/North
   Pole using dogsleds and canoes.
2. six voyagers from Russia, Japan, Great Britain,
   Denmark, and the United States
3. across the Arctic Ocean
4. March–July, 1994
5. challenge, educational application, investigate,
   pollution advances
6. tandem—one in front of the other
   rendezvous—a meeting
7. Answers will vary.

More Adventures page 48

Answers will vary.

Adventure Matchup page 49

1.	d	7.	c
2.	k	8.	a
3.	f	9.	i
4.	e	10.	l
5.	g	11.	h
6.	b	12.	j

From the Animals page 51

1.	goat	6.	dog
2.	chicken	7.	chicken
3.	yak	8.	cat
4.	pig	9.	horse
5.	cat	10.	cow

Say What? page 52

1.	d, b	7.	c, a
2.	c, d	8.	a, d
3.	a, d	9.	b, a
4.	d, b	10.	c, d
5.	d, a		
6.	d, a		

It's Yukigassen Time! page 53

1. a. win 2 periods
   b. flag snatch or more "living" fighters
2. 9 minutes, time it takes to capture 1 flag, 2 periods
3. Answers will vary.
4. the categories of the prizes

Spring to Life! page 54

1.	d	5.	a
2.	g	6.	f
3.	b	7.	c
4.	e		
8.	F		
9.	T		
10.	T		
11.	F		

12. Persephone returns to her mother each spring.

We Are Their World page 55

1.	organism	7.	parasite
2.	colony	8.	germs
3.	antibodies	9.	habitat
4.	microbe	10.	dust mite
5.	pathogens	11.	amoeba
6.	plaque	12.	toxins

Measure for Measure page 56

1. A bushel equals four pecks.
2. Walk two steps, and you have a pace.
3. A palm is the measure across four fingers of your
   hand.
4. A byte holds eight bits of memory.
5. The English ell is 45 inches long.
6. An are is comprised of one hundred square meters.
7. A cubit is the distance from fingertip to elbow.
8. A year is the time it takes the earth to orbit the sun.
9. The width of one's thumb became one inch.
10. A digit is the width of one's finger.
11. A Roman mile was a thousand paces.
12. A league equals three miles.
13. A liter of water weighs one kilogram.
14. A light year is approximately six trillion miles.

True Stories from The Sea   **page 57**
Keep Out of the Light
The Cadillac of Fish
What Big Eyes You Have!
Dill Pickle
Breathe Deeply

Northern Language   **page 58**
1. boat
2. knife
3. cow
4. Iceland
5. brooch
6. coin
7. Normandy
8. ski
9. Valhalla
10. fish
11. runes
12. Thor
13. turf
14. barley

The Explorers   **page 59**
1. a. journals—written records
   b. Carthage—famous colony
   c. Lebanon—land of ancient Phoenicia
   d. Hanno—admiral
   e. baboons—hairy savages
   f. Morocco—where six colonies were established
2. excellent sailors and explorers
3. Morocco—western coast of Africa

Turn the Radio On   **page 60**
1. The information is in order as follows:
   1. born
   2. private education
   3. read article
   4. two miles
   5. British navy
   6. Atlantic Ocean
2. The information is in order as follows:
   1. Livorno
   2. Heinrich
   3. patent
   4. English Channel
   5. Nobel
   6. died
3. Answers will vary. One example is Guglielmo Marconi invented an early radio.

Fantastic Fungi   **page 61**
1. B
2. R
3. E
4. A
5. D
6. O
7. R
8. I
9. S
10. E
Puzzle: Bread to rise

A Word Within Words   **page 62**
1. butcher
2. butte
3. butternut
4. Butte
5. rebuttal
6. butter
7. halibut
8. abut
9. button
10. butt
11. butterfly
12. debut
13. butterscotch
14. butane
15. peanut butter
16. buttercup
17. butler
18. buttress

Ferdinand Magellan   **page 64**
1. a route to the Spice Islands and proof that it was Spanish
2. to avoid war
3. killed by Philippine warriors
4. Answers will vary but may include hunger, spies, hostile nations, worms.
5. cloves

6. attractive
7. suppress
8. sail around

Sir Francis Drake, the "Sea Dog"   **page 66**
1. an English sea captain, military commander, buccaneer, sea dog, explorer, and knight.
2. She gave her support, money, and ships.
3. a pirate
4. English sea captains who sailed during the rule of Queen Elizabeth I
5. Answers will vary.
6. San Francisco—c
   Mexican port—d
   John Hawkins—e
   Golden Hind—f
   Cacafuego—a
   "El Draque"—b
7. Answers will vary.
8. His travels helped the British by increasing trade and bringing knowledge of the world.
9. c
10. Answers will vary.

Lights, Camera, Action!   **page 68**
1. a. plant from which Egyptians made boats
   b. could only propel with the wind
   c. one who steered the ship
   d. an ancient land in eastern Africa
   e. the only female pharaoh
2. Report 1—ship construction
   Report 2—ship job
   Report 3—trade
3. Report 1—bundles, stern, float
   Report 2—oarsman, rudder, cargo
   Report 3—sacrifice, myrrh, exotic

Amazing Animals   **page 69**
1. S—the smallest mammal
2. P—may live to be 100 years old
3. R—its young is called a squab
4. A—can stay in the air for months without rest
5. Y—produces caviar, an expensive food
6. B—fastest animal in the world
7. L—a group of these is called a down
8. O—besides humans, the best maker of tools
9. O—spends most of its life upside down
10. D—heaviest snake
11. F—belongs to the animal group annelids
12. R—has the largest eyes of all animals
13. O—simplest animal form
14. M—a fish with the largest eggs
15. E—can produce 188 decibels of sound
16. Y—the only bird known to attack and kill humans
17. E—ate stones because it didn't chew well

Puzzle: Spray blood from corners of its eyes

Awesome Sites   **page 71**
1. Tenochtitlán, Cave of Ten Thousand Buddhas, Krak des Chevaliers
2. to honor Buddha, a fortress for soldiers, city for the Aztecs

3. images carved into wall, Aztec sun god, conflict between Christians and Muslims, prince from India, floating islands of Tenochtitlán, a structure thought to be impregnable
4. the cave and fortress

On the Fly page 72
1. O—royal
2. U—strenuous
3. R—perceptive
4. M—gulp
5. U—secure
6. S—trifle
7. C—elegant
8. L—adventure
9. E—ecstasy
10. S—serene
11. A—sob
12. R—cease
13. E—insignia
14. N—storm
15. O—container
16. T—bunch
17. S—flounder
18. T—saturate
19. R—vivid
20. O—race
21. N—stationery
22. G—wilt
23. E—core
24. N—swivel
25. O—theme
26. U—quiver
27. G—gleeful
28. H—shelter
Puzzle: Our muscles are not strong enough.

Don't Mind If I Do page 73
1. e
2. c
3. h
4. n
5. b
6. l
7. f
8. i
9. j
10. a
11. m
12. d
13. g
14. k

To Be or Not to Be page 74
1. it neared extinction.
2. naturalists remove the second.
3. additional refuges have been made along the route.
4. numbers do not rise quickly.
5. so a new flock was made.
6. the number of cranes dropped from 600 to 16.

Achievements and Discoveries page 75
Battuta—1350, crossed Sahara, Arab
Coronado—1540, discovered Grand Canyon, Spanish
Cousteau—1943, invented Aqua-Lung, French
Gagarin—1961, orbited the earth, Soviet
Hedin—1900, mapped Central Asia, Swedish

Getting Out of Danger page 76
beluga—Canada, established park
desert tortoise—Mohave, removed fence
golden lion tamarin—Brazil, captive breeding

Komodo dragon—Indonesia, tourism
pronghorn—Wyoming, stopped motorcycle race

The Wright Stuff page 77
1. Wilbur
2. newspaper, bicycle manufacture and repair
3. an $18-dollar bike
4. sand dunes, pastures
5. Orville
6. curious, stubborn, mechanical, organized
7. They wouldn't let others photograph their work.

Another Moses? page 78
1. A
2. B
3. D
4. C
5. C
6. D
7. B
8. A
9. B
10. C
11. D
12. A
13. B
14. C
15. D
16. A
17. C
18. A
19. D
20. C
21. A
22. D
23. B

Birthday Doubles page 79
1. Paul Revere, J. Edgar Hoover
2. Lewis Carroll, Wolfgang Mozart
3. Judy Blume, Abraham Lincoln
4. Queen Elizabeth II, Tony Danza
5. Patrick Henry, Bob Hope
6. George Bush, Anne Frank
7. Kristi Yamaguchi, Bill Cosby
8. Amelia Earhart, Simón Bolívar
9. Mahatma Gandhi, Groucho Marx
10. Louisa May Alcott, Madeleine L'Engle
11. Jonathan Swift, Mark Twain
12. Tiger Woods, Sandy Koufax

Julius Caesar page 81
1. publicized victories, married daughter of a leader, planned social events, became a gifted speaker, was made a priest
2. noble
3. political group who tried to please the city's poor
4. only in emergencies
5. an official celebration of a general's victory
6. male, law-making, wealthy
7. They thought their power had been stolen.
8. brazen

Hitch Your Wagon to a Star page 82
1. fail miserably, an attempt to be perfect for a day
2. mum's the word, tell no one the secret
3. take a shine to, young girl for her new kitten
4. to punish severely, Aunt Polly when she found out Tom had gone swimming
5. par for the course, fireworks on Independence Day
6. skillful and alert, what one would hope of a pilot
7. can't hold a candle to, hot dog to T-bone

Up Above My Head page 84
1. *ISS*—1998, a science lab orbiting the earth
NEAR—1996, probe the Eros asteroid
SOHO—1995, study the sun's activities
Galileo—1989, examine Jupiter and its moons
2. spot in space where the gravitational pulls of the sun and the earth are equal.

3. Russia's space program was on hold during civil unrest.
4. Deep Impact
5. Answers will vary.

Famous People page 85

1.	f	6.	d
2.	e	7.	b
3.	n	8.	j
4.	a	9.	c
5.	i	10.	g

1. James Thurber
2. Gloria Steinem
3. Jonathan Swift
4. Paul Dickson
5. Charles Dickens
6. Elayne Boosler
7. Erma Bombeck
8. George Ade
9. David Letterman
10. Peter DeVries
11. Yogi Berra
12. Jeff Valdez
13. C.S. Lewis
14. Joel Chandler Harris
15. Winston Churchill

The Lady with the Lamp page 87
1. an English gentlewoman
2. Her family disapproved
3. filthy, poorly staffed
4. train as a nurse
5. call for assistance
6. The wealthy seldom
7. worked as a nurse . . . in Turkey
8. Florence walked 4 miles every night
9. a food-service elevator
10. war between Russia and France/Turkey/England
11. Florence wrote about nursing and hospital design
12. because he complained, English soldiers finally got treatment

What Is Power? page 89
1. Amenhotep
2. Aye
3. Amon
4. the old capital city dedicated to the sun god
5. "he who is beneficial to Aton"
6. a royal craftsman
7. employed
8. "desired," "asked for"
9. no
10. He tried to begin a new religion, but the priests of Amon were too strong.
11. Answers will vary.

Feel the Force page 90
1. a. produces, b. light
2. c. rapid, d. exceeds
3. e. natural, f. matter
4. g. force, h. turn
5. i. temperature, j. liquid
6. k. generating, l. sun
7. m. shaped, n. moving
8. o. device, p. strike
9. q. space, r. by
10. s. material, t. current

Weather 'Tis Nobler page 91
1. Aurora Borealis
2. rainbow
10. sirocco
11. precipitation

3. desert
4. fog
5. cumulus
6. cyclone
7. jet stream
8. tornado
9. satellite
12. meteorology
13. sleet
14. monsoon
15. squall
16. downpour
17. acid rain
18. El Niño

Puzzle: barometric pressure

Franklin Facts page 92
1. he sent him to work for an older son
   A Loving Father
2. Deborah Read is unable to marry Ben Franklin.
   A Lost Husband
3. Franklin instituted a number of firefighting companies for Philadelphia.
4. Franklin traveled far along the Eastern coast of the American colonies
   Improving the Mail
5. Ben regretted that he had not had the boy inoculated
   A Parent Grieves
6. Franklin accidentally shocked himself, knocking himself unconscious for several minutes
   An Electric Shock
7. Franklin wrote an attack on the white frontiersman who had killed these helpless victims
   Uncovering Murder
8. he wrote, "Gentlemen, we must now all hang together, or we shall most assuredly hang separately."
   Banding Together
9. Franklin sailed to France
   Finding Financial Aid
10. Franklin was puzzled
   Liberty for All

Anne Frank's Flight page 94
1. Anne Frank
2. They hid from soldiers, were discovered, and sent to concentration camps.
3. Hitler was creating anti-Jewish laws in Germany.
4. a. Amsterdam, b. secret annex
5. They were Jews.
6. They had to stay silent during the day; conditions were cramped and difficult.
7. writing in her diary
8–10. Answers will vary.

Get into Focus page 95

1.	3, 2, 4, 1	8.	1, 3, 2, 4
2.	1, 3, 4, 2	9.	2, 3, 1, 4
3.	1, 4, 2, 3	10.	4, 3, 2, 1
4.	3, 2, 1, 4		
5.	1, 3, 2, 4		
6.	2, 1, 4, 3		
7.	2, 3, 1, 4		

Sharpen the Focus page 96

1.	1, 2, 4, 3	6.	1, 3, 4, 2
2.	4, 2, 3, 1	7.	1, 4, 2, 3
3.	2, 3, 4, 1	8.	4, 3, 1, 2
4.	4, 1, 3, 2	9.	3, 1, 4, 2
5.	2, 3, 4, 1	10.	2, 1, 4, 3

The Battlefield Angel
page 97

1821—born
1829—boarding school
1832–1834—cares for brother
1838—teaches
1857—suffers from malaria
1861–1865—nurses
1865—visits prison
1870—learns of Red Cross
1872—returns to States
1876—recovers
1880—American Red Cross
1891—Russian aid
1904—retires from Red Cross
1912—dies

Facts About Japan
page 98

1. L	6. W	11. C
2. W	7. C	12. W
3. C	8. W	13. C
4. P	9. P	14. C
5. P	10. P	15. C

An Ancient Land
page 99

1. W	6. C	11. W
2. P	7. C	12. W
3. C	8. C	13. W
4. C	9. W	14. C
5. L	10. P	15. C

Bears Compared
page 100

1. Answers will vary.
2. Adult males are usually longer and heavier than females.
3. Diagram should display contrasts in habitat, appearance, and habits. Comparisons should include living in dens, some food, similarities, etc.
4. Answers will vary.

Norse Traditions
page 101

1. 2	10. 4	
2. 4	11. 5	
3. 4	12. 2	
4. 5	13. 1	
5. 1	14. 3	
6. 3	15.	no pockets
7. 2	16.	use tents
8. 5	17.	Midgard
9. 4	18.	circular
	19.	farming

A Pioneer Childhood
page 102

1. Love of reading
   witty
   friendly
   love of words
2. Because few people owned books; because few people lived nearby.
3. A respect for education.
4. Two-faced.

State Your Case
page 103

1. 　　　　W Y O M I N G
2. 　　M I C H I G A N
3. 　　　　　N E W Y O R K
4. 　　　　I L L I N O I S
5. 　　　　A R I Z O N A
6. 　　　A L A B A M A
7. 　　　M A I N E
8. 　　M I S S O U R I
9. 　　　　　U T A H
10. 　K E N T U C K Y
11. N E W H A M P S H I R E
12. 　　　C A L I F O R N I A
13. 　　　T E X A S
14. 　　　　　C O L O R A D O
15. 　　　　N E W J E R S E Y

Woolly Mammoth
page 104

Change the following words:
thin to *thick*, eliminate *Hawaii* and *South America*, *Industrial* to *Ice*, add *not* to *was* (was not first form of elephant), *wide* to *tall*, *pounds* to *tons*, *months* to *years*, *no specimen* to *some specimen*, *carnivore* to *herbivore* or *plant eater*, *tails* to *tusks*, *hot* to *cold*, and *summer* to *winter*

Knightly Words
page 105

1. lance
2. chain mail
3. joust
4. cavalry
5. manor
6. crest
7. squire
8. visor
9. moat
10. dubbing
11. chivalry
12. falconer

What's the Point?
page 106

1. Magnificent promises are not always matched by performance.
2. One can change one's appearance but not one's nature.
3. Too much cunning can have unfortunate results.
4. It is a great art to do the right thing at the right time.

Silent Sentinels
page 109

1. the eruptions of three volcanoes
2. the Polynesians
3. about A.D. 400
4. 2,200 miles west of Chile in the South Pacific
5. Each clan would send a young man swimming to the tern's nesting ground. The clan leader who first received his swimmer's captured egg became birdman.
6. moai
7. Answers will vary.
8. One thousand islanders were enslaved and sent to Peru. Survivors infected remaining islanders with smallpox.
9. Rapa Nui

Cave Life   page 110
1. discover
2. erupts, cool, leaving
3. scoop, rock
4. time, earth, through
5. demand, obtain, sprout
6. species, see, sensors
7. only, bat, young

Must Be Santa   page 111
1. Lycia
2. bishop
3. Constantine
4. December 6
5. wooden shoes
6. Sint Nikolass
7. *The Night Before Christmas*
8. cartoonist
9. Answers will vary.

Idioms   page 112
1. eat humble pie
2. sell for a song
3. talk in circles
4. out of whack
5. dime a dozen
6. get into a stew
7. on pins and needles
8. throw in the towel
9. catch 40 winks
10. lick one's chops
11. barking up the wrong tree

Punxsutawney Phil   page 113
1. to look for food
2. because there were no badgers
3. badgers
4. the Germans
5. trustworthy
6. no
7. 72%
8. Answers will vary.

Historically Speaking   page 114
1. solemnly, execute, preserve
2. fellow, America, freedom
3. score, conceived, and proposition
4. acutely, President, ballots
5. brace, duties, finest
6. insure, welfare, ordain
7. course, liberty, death
8. Chiefs, sick, forever

Lucky Charms   page 116
1. with a split hoof
2. pants
3. for good luck
4. "let it be so" or "I hope"
5. because lightning struck oaks so often

A Crown of Wild Olive Leaves   page 117
1. male   7. weights
2. site   8. him
3. seen   9. toes
4. way   10. won
5. sent   11. all
6. wore   12. thrown
Student sentences will vary.

Food! Glorious Food!   pages 119–120
1. d   4. c
2. b   5. b
3. d   6. c